To Linda,
with best wishes.

C000182596

The Meaning
is in the Shadows

Peter McVerry SJ

VERITAS

Published 2003 by
Veritas Publications
7/8 Lower Abbey Street
Dublin 1
Email publications@veritas.ie
Website www.veritas.ie

Thanks to: *The Evening Herald* for permission to reprint 'In the Midst of the Celtic Tiger' as the introduction to this book; *The Irish Catholic* for permission to reprint 'Responding to Homelessness'; *The Furrow* for permission to reprint 'Homelessness'; *The Messenger* for permission to reprint 'For The Almighty Has Done Great Things for Me'; *Redemptorist Publications/Reality* for permission to reprint 'The Crossing of Life', 'The Prisoner', 'Irish Prisons', 'Just a Ten Year Old Poor Kid', 'A Tale of Two Sisters', 'Gardaí', 'Why Was Jesus Executed?', 'Joyriders', 'Forgiveness is The Soul of Justice', 'A Question of Rights', 'Unaffordable Housing – a cancer in our society', 'Heroin – Agony or Ecstasy or Both?' and 'The Scandal of All Scandals'; *The Marino Institute of Education* for permission to reprint 'Prophets in the Educational System', *The Institute of Public Administration* for permission to reprint 'Homelessness and Exclusion' and *Liffey Press* for permission to reprint 'Towards a Just Society'.

ISBN 978 1 85390 731 9

10 9 8 7 6 5 4 3

A catalogue record for this book is available from the British Library.

Cover design by Pierce Design
Printed in the Republic of Ireland by ColourBooks Ltd, Dublin

Veritas books are printed on paper made from the wood pulp of managed forests. For every tree felled, at least one tree is planted, thereby renewing natural resources.

Contents

Foreword

With time you come to realise that the struggle for faith and the struggle for justice have much in common, though perhaps the reference to struggle in both cases may well surprise and indeed offend some. Nevertheless life has taught me that all of the deepest of our desires and challenges are formed out of struggle and are never fully resolved.

Certainty in faith is a bit like certainty in love. It feels good for a while, but as you begin to live with it questions inevitably arise. Or at least they should, because both faith and love are only to really be exercised in freedom and without uncertainty there can surely be no freedom. The price of our freedom and thus of our ability to really love must surely be the ongoing pain of uncertainty. So we struggle with our faith and we struggle with our doubt. Sometimes our faith reassures us; on occasions it can really support us; as often though it can leave us feeling that we are dangling in the wind of a profound uncertainty. Oftentimes too, some of its practitioners can offend us and hurt us. Faith is a a perpetual challenge; it is probably also a perpetual affront.

It is easier to say the same thing about justice. We know it is desirable. We preach by word and deed in its favour, but sometimes we are not perhaps too clear what we mean by it. We do of course want an end to the extreme manifestations of injustice – the people sleeping on the streets, the old people in pain on hospital trolleys, the teenager shooting up heroin, the travellers camped on the side of the road. But is it our sense of injustice that is challenged or our sense of the aesthetic? Poor education, institutionalised inequality, poor housing in crime-ridden estates run by effectively absentee local authority landlords, scandalous school drop-out rates, and, above all, the virtual certainty that being born into poverty guarantees that you will die in poverty, are all manifestations of an injustice more extensive than that which offends our eyes. How would we react if it was all made invisible, if the homeless were all banished to the remoter suburbs as one official proposed, if heroin abuse was confined to communities through whom we never had to travel, and if the Travellers were 'moved on'. If our streets sparkled brightly would our consciences rest easy? Perhaps we would like it to, but many of us would find it difficult.

There is always a prophet to challenge us, to push us to deeper reflection and indeed to remind us of what we claim to believe. And we all believe. Some of us are socialists, some of us are Christians, some of us claim to be both! For all of us there are prophets who challenge us. Peter McVerry is one of those who makes our lives uncomfortable. Like my great and sadly deceased friend Frank O'Leary, he has a way of demolishing our excuses – though it is often after the event that we realise just how fragile our excuses were!

Peter was my first introduction to the Jesuits. And we had barely met when I started an argument about schools and elitism which he took firmly and gently in his stride. His life in the thirty subsequent years is probably his best answer to my challenges, without a doubt a better testimony to faith and justice than my own. For people who know Peter McVerry his life is both the challenge and the inspiration, and this is reflected in this book.

But of course it doesn't give us final answers because the struggle for faith and the struggle for justice are precisely that, struggles which challenge us throughout our lives. Struggle is hard, thankless and often unsuccessful. Many, understandably, give up. Others of us have the fortune (I'm not sure whether I should say good or mis-!) to collide with prophets, and, like Jeremiah, we may sometimes lament, but we can't give up.

Brendan Ryan
Senator
Dáil Éireann

Introduction:
In the Midst of the Celtic
Tiger

The skyline reveals the amazing changes that have taken place in Irish society in recent years. Cranes, cranes and more cranes reveal the frantic expansion in the construction industry as it tries to meet the demand of a flourishing economy.

Lower down, traffic snarl-ups are frustrating evidence of a consumer demand which is being readily met. Everywhere we look, the evidence of increased prosperity stares us in the face.

Well, not quite everywhere. In the shadows, almost invisible in the darkness, there are other lives which have barely changed.

Like Donal, a schizophrenic, who is totally incapable of living independently, who cuts his arms with a razor, who burns himself with cigarettes, who will only wash and change his clothes under persistent pressure, and who was admitted to the psychiatric ward of a Dublin hospital. Two weeks later, he was discharged, as his bed in the acute ward was required by another patient, and there was no other suitable accommodation which he could be offered. He was given a note for the Homeless Persons Unit, stating that he was homeless and in need of emergency accommodation. Living on the streets for anyone is misery, for a person like Donal, it is hell. Life in the shadows is tough.

Like Frank, homeless, in the care of the Health Board, who had been accessing accommodation on a nightly basis, from the emergency overnight social work service. On the night of his eighteenth birthday, he went, as usual, to the emergency service only to be told that since he was now eighteen, he was no longer eligible for the service. He 'celebrated' the night of his eighteenth birthday in a doorway. He is still on the streets. Adulthood in the shadows.

Like John, with a long history of physical and sexual abuse as a child, who started taking drugs at fourteen years old to suppress the painful memories. His mother was usually too drunk to care. The only time he felt any happiness was the few hours after he had injected heroin – the past faded into oblivion, the future became irrelevant, only the present moment with its buzz and pleasant feelings was real. He needed therapy, but there was a three month wait for a methadone programme and then a much longer wait for residential treatment where the therapy might begin. He could no longer face the pain of waking up sick each morning, the pain of having to go out robbing for his drugs, the pain of always having to lie and to manipulate. Nor could he face the prospect, without therapy, of becoming drug-free and remembering. Remembering what he had spent years trying to forget. Last month, he killed himself. In the shadows, things are often not what they appear to be – life is sometimes death and death is always life.

Everyone was too busy making money, too busy spending money, to notice John and Frank and Donal suffering in the shadows. And the politicians were too busy helping everyone to make even more money, and helping everyone to spend even more money, to notice John and Frank and Donal in the shadows.

But their painful memories of the past, and painful experiences of the present, and expectations of an equally painful future were pains they could tolerate; the much deeper pain was the pain of knowing that nobody cared. As they look up at the cranes ceaselessly turning in the sky, and out at the traffic as it rushes by, and at the people elbowing each other for room in the shopping centres, the feeling that no-one even notices their plight – that is the feeling that hurts most. For them, life is about being born, suffering, and then dying. It has no meaning. Their lives are of no value to anyone, they have no significance for anyone else, everyone is too busy to care. They know that if they disappeared off the face of the earth, no-one would even notice that they had gone.

Most of those in the shadows are unaware that they are, in fact, God's favourites; that Jesus too came and lived in the shadows. He too experienced the rejection, the misunderstanding and the suffering imposed (or not taken away) for reasons of political expediency. God became one of them.

And most of us, as we rush to work, to play or to spend, and seek to find security for our children in our assets and bank balances, sometimes we pause to try and find meaning in it all. The hassle, the stress, the rush – what is it all for? We ask the politicians and they tell us that the meaning is in the activity itself; we ask the Churches and we are told to search in a different world. We search here, we search there, but we cannot find an answer that satisfies our deeper selves. We look deep into ourselves, we look up at the sky, we look to the East (no point in looking to the West) but the meaning of all this frantic activity eludes us.

Of course it does. Because the meaning is in the shadows.

The Bad Old Days
are Here to Stay

My life totally changed on September 11th. On September 11th
1974, that is. On that day, I went with two other Jesuits to live in a
flat in a tenement building in Summerhill, in the north inner city
of Dublin.

Why did we go there? We weren't at all sure – it just seemed
like a good idea at the time. In those years, the middle of the
1970s, the Jesuits were trying to rediscover their roots and their
mission, and that new understanding was being expressed in the
phrase 'the service of the faith and the promotion of justice'. As
part of that mission, there was an awareness of the need to engage
much more with people living on the margins, and this gave rise
to an emphasis on the importance of 'inserted communities',
groups of Jesuits living with those who were poor. In Ireland, as
elsewhere, we felt the need to establish this sort of community. It
was only later that we really realised why we had gone there.

For me, the move was an enormous shock. I had no idea of the
conditions that existed there. Fortunately, the day we moved in it
wasn't raining. When it rained, the rain came through the ceiling.
We were some of the lucky ones – it all came together in the
middle of the room and dripped down from the light bulb; for
others, whole rooms became unusable. And the rats, the place was
crawling with rats, rats the size of little kittens, immune to every
poison that had ever been invented. Again, we were lucky; our flat
was on the top floor of the house. As we lay in bed at night, you
could hear the rats, all night long, crawling in the ceiling, fighting

one another, squealing, dragging bits of food, sometimes gnawing through the electric wires. But families on the ground floor would often talk about waking up in the morning and finding a rat on the baby's cot! Worst of all was the soundproofing – there wasn't any. Originally, these houses were each occupied by one family; eight rooms, two on each floor, making a very substantial home for a wealthy family. However, when the inner city began to decline, these families moved out to the suburbs and Dublin Corporation purchased the houses. Each house was made into eight flats. Eight families, some of them with six or eight or ten children, now occupied what was originally one family home. In our flat, we could hear the news on the television in the flat below. You could hear every word of their conversations. But it got worse! Because Summerhill was used by Dublin Corporation as a 'dumping ground' for families with problems (although many very fine families also lived there), each house had at least one such 'problem' family. Frequently, the family's problem was drink. Typically, the parents would return from the pub at one or two in the morning and sometimes they would have an almighty row. They would be shouting at one another, cursing, arguing; throwing things at one another which would smash against the wall or fly out through the window; the children could be heard crying. Because of the absence of any soundproofing, these rows kept the other seven families awake. Maybe two or three times a week, every family in the house would be forced to listen to one family's problems for hours on end, always in the early hours of the morning. Sleep was just as scarce as food for many children.

I was shocked at the conditions in which so many people had to live. But I was also appalled at the realisation that I had lived in Dublin for many years, and for several of those years I had lived less than a quarter of a mile away from Summerhill, and never knew that such conditions existed.

I grew up in a very privileged family. We lived in Newry, a small town just across the border in Northern Ireland. My father was a doctor, so we were very comfortably off and the social status of a doctor in a small Irish town was extremely high. I went to a fee-paying boarding school, as my father had before me, and the limits of my world were defined by the people I associated with and the lifestyle I enjoyed. My noviceship with the Jesuits was spent in a large country home set in the middle of a forest. I attended university while living in a castle, no less, in an affluent suburb of Dublin. I studied philosophy and theology living in an enormous building in the most prestigious district of Dublin. I was horrified, therefore, not only at the conditions that I found in Summerhill, but at my total ignorance of this other world that existed only minutes from where I had lived in blissful serenity. I learnt that to live a privileged life, you also had to live a sheltered life. Awareness makes the privileged life too uncomfortable.

That blissful serenity was disturbed on September 11th 1974. It was later shattered completely. I soon learnt that the conditions in which people lived were not the main problem. Summerhill was on a main route for motorists coming into the city in the morning, to work or to shop, and then back out again to the suburbs in the evening. Car after car after car passing by these tenement buildings, morning after morning after morning, all as equally ignorant as myself at the life that teemed and struggled behind the communal front door. But what was the message that these motorists unwittingly gave to the residents there? Well, the message that the residents picked up was that they were of no importance, their lives and sorrows and struggles were of no concern, their existence was irrelevant. Every morning, the residents of Summerhill experienced, not just the hardship of life on the margins, but also the indignity of feeling that nobody gave a damn. And every evening, the experience was repeated. The struggle in Summerhill was not just to survive – and some didn't – but to survive with dignity. Those in Summerhill, like millions in poverty around our world, were the *real* defenders of human rights as they struggled to affirm their dignity in the face of relentless and persevering opposition.

After a short while, we realised that one of the urgent unmet needs was that of the children. Most of the children had left school early, some at nine or ten years of age; they were hanging around the streets; they had no money in their pockets so they invariably started robbing; they ended up in jail. Going to jail was, for some, just as inevitable, just as much part of their life, as going to third-level education was for others. I sometimes visited three generations of the same family in prison together – mother and daughter, or father and son, sharing the same prison cell, the grandfather, in deference to his age, having a cell of his own. These were kids with no fear. I watched in horror as children climbed drainpipes to get into their flat on the fourth floor, because their mother was out and they didn't know when she would return. While other children (foolishly) poured petrol on their Halloween bonfire to get a better effect, these kids used a full petrol tank with car attached, oblivious to, or uncaring of, the danger. We began working with the children.

It was not very long before I was questioning everything I had, for so long, taken for granted. I thought I knew right from wrong. Robbing what belonged to another was wrong, there was little need for any discussion of the issue. But here were kids who could never afford to buy a new pair of jeans robbing a pair from a large department store, which made millions of pounds in profit every year to be distributed amongst the shareholders who were already very comfortably off. I was not able to condemn these kids. What was right and what was wrong?

They would get arrested for shoplifting or burglary and get a hiding in the garda station. *Two* crimes would be committed, one a larceny, the other a violent assault on a young person. But the assault was never prosecuted while the larceny was. The kid went to jail for shoplifting, but no-one went to jail for leaving him bruised and sore. The kid was branded a criminal for life, the garda was considered an upstanding, respected member of society. Where was right and wrong?

Even worse, the gardaí are rightly understood to be defenders of society; their role is to ensure the safety and security of that society. So when a garda batters a kid from Summerhill, the kid understands that it is *society* that is doing it to him. When a garda calls a kid a 'scumbag', it is *society* that calls him that. I thought my job was to instil into these young people a respect for society and for the laws of society – now I saw that I was wasting my breath, unless I could *first* instil into society a respect for these kids. I never understood why someone would maliciously damage public property, smash a telephone, uproot a young, recently planted, tree, smash public lighting – *now* I understand the alienation that produces such incidents.

A kid broke into a house and stole a young couple's life savings, which they had been putting aside to pay a deposit on a house. The young couple were devastated, their dream of getting out of their unsatisfactory accommodation into a new house was shattered. Of course, what the kid did was wrong and even living in poverty does not make it right. But I thought of land speculators, who, with the support and encouragement of politicians, made vast profits by doing nothing and in the process shattered many a young couple's dream of buying their own home. We condemn the kid, but the land speculator is a respected member of society. One broke the law, the other didn't – but in both cases the young couple ended up in the same plight. Who makes the laws, I had to ask myself? Who decides what is right and what is wrong? Certainly not the kid.

A kid broke into a house while the occupants were out at work and robbed the money that was to buy the food and pay the bills for the rest of the week, until the next payday. The family he had robbed would, as a result, have to go hungry or borrow money to make ends meet. But the kid's family lived on a social welfare payment – decided by the Government – which ensured that *every week* they would go hungry or have to borrow money to make ends meet, money that they could never repay. I wondered why was one wrong, and the other right.

These kids robbed (before drugs in the 1980s began to dominate their lives) in order to have what the rest of us take for granted – decent clothes, proper food, a nice home, a night out, a few days away. I began to wonder why does our society condemn them *without also, and equally,* condemning the obscene wealth and exorbitant incomes that others in our society enjoy?

These young people had their own moral code. Robbing Dunnes Stores was OK, robbing an old person was not. You don't rob your own. You rob the rich, you don't rob the poor. Like all of us, they sometimes didn't live up to their own moral code. But they knew right from wrong, only it wasn't the same as *my* right and wrong. And sometimes they got it wrong – if you own a car or your own house, you must be rich, therefore you can be robbed. But they didn't appreciate that a person may be spending all their wages on a mortgage or a car loan. Perhaps this was outside their range of comprehension, as they could never, in a month of Sundays, get a mortgage or a loan, except from some 'loan shark' who was robbing them with an exorbitant and illegal rate of return, but there was nothing they could do about it.

These kids saw no other way of living a decent life, except by crime. And for most of them, there *was* no other way. The jobs on which they, and their parents, and their grandparents, depended were unskilled manual labour, particularly on the docks. But with containerisation, and in the wider economy with increased technology, the need for unskilled labour was rapidly disappearing. Education was not a high priority in that culture; reading and writing were necessary to survive in life (and even writing for many became an obsolete skill through lack of practice) but learning French or calculus or the names of the rivers of Russia (wherever that might be) was going to be of little use on a building site or shovelling grain out of the hold of a boat. And so when education became the only game in town, they were left behind. Crime was all that was left to them. Whole families lived on crime; parents profited from the crimes of their children; children felt valued by their contribution to the family. Real entrepreneurial skills and teamwork were revealed. In icy weather, when cars had difficulty in getting up the hill in Gardiner Street, they would offer to push your car – for a price! Everyone paid – nobody was going to risk having to abandon their car in Gardiner Street! One young lad stood at the pedestrian traffic lights in Summerhill; another was on the rooftop examining the cars that were approaching. When he saw a car with a female occupant and the handbag lying on the front seat, a signal to press the button on the traffic lights was given to the kid below. When the car dutifully stopped, a third young lad, with his face covered, ran out of the flats, broke the window, grabbed the bag and ran back again into the flats, down to the basement which ran continuously along the whole street and provided a perfect escape route. The only identifiable youth, the one at the traffic lights, could not be arrested, as there was no evidence of him being involved in the crime. Later, the three would divide the spoils.

While crime was an occupation for some, 'joyriding' was an expression of who they were. The playground at the rear of

Summerhill taught many a twelve year old how to drive. The kids drove past garda cars in their stolen vehicles and beeped the horn, hoping to get a chase. *Starsky and Hutch* was the police series that everyone was glued to – it featured, for its day, spectacular police chases. But it paled into dullness compared to looking out the window of the flats in Summerhill.

And what were they saying, these 'joyriders'? They were saying: 'I'm not nobody, I'm somebody'. They were trying to convince, first themselves, but also the rest of society. The message they were receiving from society was overwhelmingly the opposite, 'You're nobody, you're nothing'. And they were screaming back at society: 'I *am* somebody'. Driving (it had to be stolen cars as they had no other means of driving) was a skill that was highly desired and valued in their own culture, as in the rest of society. Driving at speed gave them a sense of achievement which they rarely otherwise experienced. And it gave them a sense of being somebody. Imagine, night after night, the evening papers devoted whole pages to their exploits earlier in the day; the politicians spent hours discussing them in the Dáil; radio and television programmes were talking about them, even interviewing them. How else could they ever have got so much attention? Everyone was talking about them. The fact that everyone else was giving out about them didn't matter, for they didn't care what everyone else thought of them. Indeed, they already knew what everyone else thought about them, which wasn't much! But they were *somebody*, at least for a while.

What they were pleading for was to be treated as somebody, *without* having to rob cars. But their pleas fell on deaf ears, nobody heard them, maybe nobody wanted to hear them. To be valued, to be cared for, to be given opportunities wasn't too much to ask for – but it wasn't given.

September 11th challenged my understanding of God. God is the one who rejoices in what is right and is crucified by what is wrong. If right and wrong are clear and obvious, then there is no confusion about whose side God is on. But when what is right and what is wrong become confused, then our image of God must change. These children were unjustly deprived of those material resources which God has given to be shared with every human being, their dignity was taken away, they were ignored and unwanted – and this was done to them by those who had authority, respect and sometimes more than their fair share of the earth's resources. These kids were doing nothing right, the rest of us were doing nothing wrong. But to believe in a God who identified with the latter and condemned the former became impossible. The kid who robbed or assaulted the elderly (an old man or woman who was made in the image and likeness of God and whose suffering God, in Jesus, identified with) had himself been robbed of his dignity and assaulted by the rest of us – and maybe by his father as well! This kid too had suffered for most of his fourteen or fifteen years. Victim and perpetrator, oppressor and oppressed, the distinction began to blur, the two images kept changing place in a kaleidoscope of movement. Whose side was God on? I began to see *myself* in that kid! I hadn't robbed or assaulted anyone, but my privileged and sheltered background, with loving parents and an excess of opportunities, was maybe more responsible for that than any moral virtue I might possess. I began to wonder, if *I* had grown up in that kid's home, and if *he* had grown up in mine, would he be the priest coming up to visit me in Mountjoy Prison? And the more I asked myself that question, the clearer the answer became. And the Gospel command: 'Do not judge and you will not be judged' jumped out of the page of the scriptures at me. Indeed, the scriptures took on a whole new meaning in this new context in which I found myself, post September 11th. And I discovered a God who is on the side of all who have to suffer, who are unwanted, cast out, robbed of their dignity. These kids, robbers and all, were very close to God's heart – God surely had a special place for them in God's Kingdom. And I wondered if I, a respectable, responsible, law-abiding and religious person, who condemned others so easily, would be looking up at them in the Kingdom from the place allocated to me in the basement!

These kids didn't believe in God, because they *couldn't* believe in God. They were taught in religion class that to rob was bad, to hurt people was bad, to damage property was bad. And since they did all that, and more, they believed that *they* were bad. If there was a God, and God knew the truth, then God was looking down at them and thinking 'There's a scumbag, I couldn't possibly love him because he is *bad, bad, bad*'. That was the message that society was giving to them all the time and the message was often reinforced by religious teaching and Sunday sermons (which they sometimes attended – there was little else to do on a Sunday morning). And so, they (rightly) concluded that it was intolerable enough to go through *life* being made to feel that you are unlovable, but the thought of having to go through *eternity* being made to feel that you are unlovable was too much to bear. And so the Good News for them was that there is *no* God – death brings an end to the pain that is inside, as well as the pain that is outside. And if these kids, who rejected the God we preached, had, as I came to believe, a very special place in God's heart, what does that say about our preaching of the Gospel for the last 2,000 years?

So now, almost thirty years later, what has changed? Well, the people are scattered – exiled to the four corners of Dublin by a deliberate decision of Dublin Corporation. These people are considered undesirable, so let's dilute them amongst the wider population, was the (unspoken, at least in public) thinking of the Corporation. The people themselves didn't want to go – they would have put up with the rats if only they could keep one another. But they had no choice – they were given no choice – their wishes were irrelevant. So they now live in houses with roofs that don't (usually) leak, the rats are (more or less) gone, and their homes are soundproofed against all but the most unholy row. But they still feel that they are on the margins, that nobody cares, that this society has no place for them. Joyriding is still a major problem for society, for these kids still have to convince themselves and the rest of us that they are somebody, not nobody. They are, some of them, staying on longer in school because they know, from experience, that today you must have at least your Junior Cert. to get the basic unskilled jobs that their parents used to get with no qualifications. It wasn't their choice to stay on in school – they never have a choice about anything – and school won't get them a *better* job, but they won't get *any* job without it. Those who rob, rob now to feed their drug habit, to stop themselves feeling sick – no longer to enjoy the lifestyle that we others take for granted. They are now doubly trapped, trapped by the lack of opportunities that this society gives them to earn a decent living, and trapped by their own addiction. Even if this society were to offer them equality of access to education and to opportunities, that, on its own, is no longer enough.

What did I do for the people of Summerhill? Probably very little. I had little to give them. They, especially the young people, got plenty of my time, they learned a few new skills, they went on a few trips away. All my philosophy and theology was irrelevant to them. They wanted their dignity as human beings to be acknowledged. I hope I was able to acknowledge that.

What did they do for me? The people of Summerhill changed me, they turned me upside down and inside out. They shattered my illusions and my complacency. They opened my eyes to what is happening in Irish society and to which I had been blind for so long. They helped me to discover a God who is passionate about the suffering of God's own children. They were God's call to me to conversion. And for that I am, for ever, grateful to them.

Homelessness

I used to think that the hardest thing about being homeless was not having a bed to sleep in – having to find a doorway, or a derelict building, or the back of an abandoned car to lay your head. But I learnt from the young people that I am working with that that is not the hardest part of being homeless. Then I thought it was being hungry or cold. But that too is not the hardest part of being homeless. So I thought it was the boredom, having nothing to do, all day, every day; walking up and down trying to pass the time. But that is not the hardest part. Now I believe that the hardest part of being homeless is to live with the knowledge that if you disappeared off the face of the earth, no-one would even notice. That defines the value of your life. You are of no value to anyone, there is no-one to whom you are important, no-one who really cares. Your life is virtually meaningless. The message you receive from society, every minute of every day, is that you are not worth the trouble or effort or expense of providing you with even a small bedsit that you can call home.

Some time ago, a homeless young man threw himself into the Liffey. When I went to see him, the next day, in hospital, he told me that he wanted to die, he couldn't just go on living like this. 'Living like what?' I said. 'I can't go on living,' he said, 'knowing that nobody cares'.

It is the loss of dignity that homeless people suffer that makes homelessness – indeed marginalisation of any description – a central issue for our Christian faith. The revelation of Jesus, that

God is the parent who loves us, has, as its corollary, that every single human being is a child of God and has the dignity of being a child of God. Where we deny that dignity to anyone, or undermine it, or threaten it, by the way in which we treat other people, then we are denying the only God that is. The dignity of every human person as a child of God is, it seems to me, the link between faith and justice. I cannot worship a God who loves me infinitely and unconditionally unless I also accept that this same God loves infinitely and unconditionally those whom I and our society would prefer to ignore.

Homelessness – both child and adult – has changed enormously since I first encountered it some twenty-five years ago. In the mid-seventies, there was no such social category as 'homeless children'. There were a small number of children who didn't live at home, but they tended to live with their granny on the next street, or with their married sister who lived a few doors away, or with the neighbour whose house they constantly visited anyway. Today, the number of homeless children is much greater – some four or five hundred each year in Dublin alone – and their granny or married sister may live on the far side of the city and they may not know their neighbours. They depend on the services of the State, which even the Minister of Health now accepts have been very far from satisfactory. Homeless children at least have a legal right to accommodation and care, under the Child Care Act, 1991. That doesn't mean that they get it. But it means that they can go to the High Court to demand accommodation and care. Even that doesn't mean that what they get is adequate. But a long procession to the High Court of homeless children, with increasingly tragic backgrounds, has caused intense embarrassment for the Government. It has revealed the true cause of homelessness, namely apathy, bureaucratic inactivity and inter-departmental fighting. It is significant that the Government Minister with responsibility for children, including homeless children (the Minister of State in the Department of Health and Children), does not even have a place at the cabinet table. The former Minister of State, Frank Fahey, subsequently promoted to Minister of the Marine, did not have a place at the cabinet table when he had responsibility for the children of Ireland; but when he became responsible for our fish, it was considered very important that he should be there.

The problem of homeless adults has changed too. Twenty-five years ago, the estimate of homeless adults in Ireland was around three thousand. They were predominantly elderly; people with an alcohol dependency; people who had been discharged from prison or the army and were so institutionalised that they could no longer live independently in the community; people who had lived and worked all their lives in England and had returned home, but had no family or friends left in Ireland. For them, the hostel was their home. That was where they put down roots. Today, the estimate is of some ten thousand homeless adults, many of them young with drug dependency, some discharged from psychiatric hospitals ('returned to the community'!), many who have 'graduated' from being homeless children to homeless adults, some of them very alienated and difficult to handle. The older homeless people moved out of the hostels and slept on the streets, as they were afraid of these newcomers. Some hostels had to impose minimum ages, twenty-five or thirty, to try and create a safe environment for the older homeless people. Young homeless people aged eighteen to twenty-five are now at crisis point. To access a bed in a hostel, they must queue by 5.30pm to have any chance. Because of the bed shortage, any attempt to assess the appropriate type of accommodation, which might suit their particular needs, is a pointless exercise. The vulnerable, recently-homeless eighteen-year-old might find him/herself sleeping (though 'sleeping' might be overstating it!) in a dormitory next to a drug user, alcoholic, sex offender or career criminal. If nobody remembered to tell him/her to sleep with their runners under their pillow, they might very well have to leave the hostel next morning in their bare feet. This is not a criticism of the staff or ethos of any particular hostel, who do a heroic job in looking after some of the roughest, toughest and most difficult homeless adults. But it is a criticism of the system, which is so inadequate even in providing emergency beds, that some homeless people become drug users or criminals because no appropriate accommodation is available to them. It takes no great imagination to appreciate what happens to the dignity of such homeless people; they have reached rock bottom and any remaining shreds of self-esteem are totally unravelled.

Homeless adults, unlike homeless children, have no legal right to accommodation or even to a bed for the night. While most of us would consider a place to live, or at least a place to spend the night, as a pretty fundamental right, no such right exists in Irish law. Indeed, in the 1980s, when the Government, under intense pressure from voluntary and religious groups, and the constant harassment of Senator Brendan Ryan, reluctantly introduced a Homeless Persons Bill, they absolutely refused to incorporate a *right in law* to accommodation for homeless Irish adults. Homeless adults thus remain dependent on the benevolence of the Minister for the Environment and the goodwill of local officials.

Where is it going? Over the next few years, we can expect to see a significant expansion in services for homeless children. After twenty years of political apathy, when it was almost impossible to interest the Government or Health Boards in the problem of homeless young people, we have moved into a phase of political panic. Getting the problem away from Justice Peter Kelly in the High Court, who has described the inertia of the Government as a 'scandal', and off the front pages of the national newspapers has become an urgent priority. With increased resources, a significant increase in the level of services can be expected. However, the problem of homeless children is not just a shortage of resources. A lack of planning, an absence of co-ordination, and a mismatch between some of the services on offer and the needs of homeless children are also significant factors. So even with increased resources, the adequacy of planning that has preceded the decision-making is dubious and hence the appropriateness of the services to be provided remains to be seen. Dealing adequately with the problem of homeless children is more important than ever, as an increasing number, not having received a proper service as children, are drifting into adult homelessness.

And with the adult homeless, the problem is all doom and gloom. The traditional exit from homelessness for them has been the private rented sector. Now, because of the price of houses, the private rented sector has become clogged with households who have to wait longer and longer for Local Authority Housing (which is clogged with households who can no longer afford a mortgage to move out into the private sector), and anyway the deposit and rents being asked for is out of the range of homeless people or people on low incomes. Hence there appears to be no way out. They are trapped on a motorway with no exits. Most of the funerals at which I officiate these days are suicides. It is difficult to see how any short or medium-term solution is possible. With record waiting lists, the Local Authorities are under intense pressure. Without a very firm commitment by Local Authorities to housing homeless people, their plight is dismal in the extreme.

I am often asked why I, as a priest, am running hostels for homeless young people. That's the job of a social worker, I am told. The implication is that I should be doing the real job of a priest, by which I presume they mean saying Mass and administering the sacraments. But if the essence of the Gospel is the proclamation that every human being has the dignity of being a child of God, then each time we affirm the dignity of someone whose dignity has been denied, we are living and preaching the gospel. To give people back their dignity, the dignity that is theirs by right as a child of God, is to proclaim the gospel, to affirm God as our Parent and to give witness to that God, just as fully as saying Mass and administering the sacraments.

In our own hostels for homeless young people, our aim is not just giving young people a bed for the night, or even feeding or clothing them. The most important objective is communicating to them that they are just as important, just as loveable, just as worth caring about as any other young person of their age. If we are not giving them this message, by the way in which we relate to them, by the way in which we involve them, then we might as well pack up and go home.

One young man who had previously lived in our hostels was serving a prison sentence. He wrote to me from prison, 'I have learnt one thing from you, that I am not such a bad person after all'. That letter summed up all that we are trying to do.

It was central to the ministry of Jesus to reach out to affirm the dignity, as children of God, of those whom his society despised, treated as second-class, and pushed to the margins, namely the infirm, the poor, the tax-collectors and the prostitutes. He affirmed their dignity in three ways:

First, he reached out to them in a preferential way. He was constantly to be found in their company so much so that 'The Pharisees and their scribes complained to Jesus' disciples and said, "Why do you eat with tax-collectors and sinners?"' (Luke 5:30)

Secondly, he challenged the values, attitudes and even the structures of his society which undermined people's dignity. 'When he arrived at the Pharisee's house and took his place at table, a woman came in who had a bad name in the town. When the Pharisee who invited him saw this, he said to himself, "If this man were a prophet, he would know who this woman is who is touching him and what a bad name she has". Then Jesus took him up and said to him: "Simon I have something to say to you."' (Luke 7:36)

Third, his affirmation of their dignity and value resulted in Jesus himself being despised and marginalised. This predicament did not result in Jesus pulling back or reconsidering his relationship with those on the margins. He continued to speak the truth and accepted the consequences.

Our response to those who are homeless can mirror Jesus' response to those on the margins of his own society.

First, we can affirm their dignity through the way in which we relate to them. I am often asked should we give money to those homeless people who are begging. I used to argue this with Senator Brendan Ryan; I used to say no, he would say yes. So I asked a young lad I knew who lived through begging. He said 'On Mondays, Tuesdays and Wednesdays, yes; on Thursdays, Fridays and Saturdays, no'. When I asked him to explain, he said that at the weekends, when people go out to pubs, night-clubs and parties, begging is very profitable – you could earn €30 an hour, far more than the minimum wage! So all the entrepreneurs come out. But on Mondays, Tuesdays and Wednesdays, the only people who beg are those who really need it! However, whether we choose to give money or not, we can always take a few seconds to have a word. To have even a brief conversation is to acknowledge them as persons, it is to affirm their dignity. A thirty-second conversation may be more important to them than a euro in the hat. I once met a man lying in the middle of the pavement. Not knowing if he was alive or dead, I went over and shook him. He turned over, and looked up at me. 'Are you alright?' I asked him. 'I am, sir,' he said, 'but thanks for asking'.

Secondly, we can seek to change the attitudes and structures which maintain homelessness. There is enormous compassion in Irish people, even in this culture of greed. But people feel powerless to influence those structures. Having spent the last twenty-five years trying more or less unsuccessfully to change the structures, I know the feeling! But we can try. A letter to the relevant Minister, expressing outrage at their plight, especially in this time of prosperity, may not seem important, but if all your friends wrote at the same time, and if all *their* friends wrote at the same time and... A little organising can produce miracles.

Thirdly, if we stand up for those who are homeless or poor or marginalised in our own communities, we might very quickly experience being despised and marginalised ourselves by those communities. Supporting a service within our neighbourhood for a group who are on the margins is a guaranteed way of discovering what it is like to be unpopular. But speaking the truth as we see it and accepting the consequences may be the right thing to do.

Homelessness anywhere is sad; homelessness in Ireland today is also obscene. Several hundred children, ten thousand adults, may sound a lot, but in Calcutta there are 250,000 homeless children alone and in Brazil there are 6 million of them. Homelessness persists not because we do not have the resources to solve it, but because we have chosen not to.

Towards a Spirituality that does Justice

In my view, having spoken to many groups in many parts of Ireland on the topic of faith and justice, the biggest obstacle to the promotion of justice is our spirituality.

Here I wish to suggest some elements of a new spirituality, or rather an adaptation of the spirituality that I have inherited, which I think are important in the promotion of justice.

In saying that our spirituality is an obstacle to the promotion of justice, I am not criticising that spirituality. That spirituality has served the Irish people well for several centuries, bringing us through the penal times and making us an extraordinarily compassionate and caring people. However, the times we live in are now very different and these different circumstances call for a different response, even at the level of faith.

We are used to different spiritualities – there is Ignatian Spirituality, Franciscan Spirituality, Dominican Spirituality and so on. The fact that I try to live an Ignatian spirituality does not mean that I consider Franciscan spirituality to be inferior. Different spiritualities are for different people at different times. Different spiritualities emerge in response to particular circumstances – what Vatican II called 'the signs of the times'. Thus Franciscan spirituality of poverty and simplicity was a response to the wealth and pomp and seeking of honours which characterised much of the Church at the time.

Today, it seems to me 'the signs of the times' suggests a new spirituality. There are two 'signs of the times' which are particularly significant:

- the first is *our awareness of the extent of poverty and marginalisation* in our world and even in our wealthy nations. This awareness, heightened as never before by technology and mass communication, makes it impossible for us not to admit that there is a situation here that needs a response, and that challenges a faith that professes a new commandment, 'love one another'.

- the second 'sign of the times' is *our awareness that this situation need not be so.* Poverty in our world, and in our separate nations, is the result of decisions that are made or not made – it is man-made, using the word 'man' quite consciously, as most of the decision-makers in our world are men. This awareness alerts us to the fact that the way things are in our world and nations can and ought to be changed. This has implications for our faith and how we respond to our faith.

I am going to highlight here seven areas where I believe that our traditional spirituality needs to be modified if we are to develop a spirituality that does justice.

What is it to be a Christian?

Traditionally, Roman Catholics have been recognised by their observance of law. A 'good' Roman Catholic is someone who does not get divorced or use artificial birth control methods, and who goes to Mass every Sunday. In the past, we added: abstains from meat on Fridays, fasts during Lent, and so on. Adherence to laws has been the defining characteristic of a Roman Catholic.

I would suggest that the defining characteristic of a Roman Catholic, or any Christian, should be our *compassion*. In the Gospel, compassion is the criterion by which we enter into or exclude ourselves from the Kingdom of God, compassion for those of God's children who are in need, or in pain. God, as parent, has, as the highest priority, the care and welfare of those of God's children who are in need. There is nothing that God, as parent, wants from us more than reaching out to those of God's children in that situation. If we do so, then God offers us everything that God possesses, namely the Kingdom. Even the cup of water given to the least of God's children will not go without its reward.

Our compassion towards those in need determines, more than anything else, God's relationship to us. It is the defining characteristic of those who profess to do what God wants and to follow Jesus.

'A new commandment I give you: love one another as I have loved you.' The *characteristic* of Christian love is its *universality*. If we exclude anyone from our love, then our love is not Christian love. It may be lofty noble ideals, or high principles, but it is not *Christian* love. If then the characteristic of Christian love is its universality, the *test* of Christian love is how well we love those we would prefer not to have to love. My love for my parents, or friends, is a part of Christian love, but it is usually the easy part. The only way of proving that my love is universal is by looking at how I love those I find it hard to love, those I despise, those I disagree with, those who have hurt me, those whom I would prefer not to have to have anything to do with.

Thus what defines us as Christian should be our compassion, our reaching out to those who are unwanted, those on the margins, those we would instinctively want to keep at arms length. When people look at us and recognise us as Christians, it ought to be because they find us reaching out to the poor, the homeless, the disabled, making those on the margins feel welcome and wanted.

The people of God

In the spirituality that I inherited, the most important thing in life was *my* relationship to God. Deepening my relationship to God, through prayer, retreats, reflection and indeed trying to live the commandment of love, was the highest priority. Here I suggest that there is something more *fundamental* (not more important, but more fundamental) than *my* relationship with God. And that is the relationship of the People of God to God. None of us goes to God on our own – we go as one of the people of God. When Yahweh made his covenant, he did not make millions of individual covenants with individual Jews, he made his covenant with the Jewish people. And Jesus called into being the new people of God, the Christian community. I go to God as one of the people of God, not just as an individual. My relationship with God exists as a part

of the relationship of the People of God to God, not independently
of it.

That means that if there is some defect in the relationship of the
people of God to God, then this affects *my* relationship to God.
Thus, even if I am in Dublin, and somebody in Cork is treating
someone else unjustly, then the relationship of the people of God to
God is not as wholesome as it should be and therefore *my*
relationship to God is not as wholesome as it should be. Like an
apple, if the apple is perfect I eat it differently than I would eat an
apple with a bad piece – the apple with the bad piece I have to be
careful of and make sure that when I get to that piece I eat carefully
around it, whereas I can eat away at the good apple with no
concerns. My relationship with the two apples is quite different!
Therefore I cannot just develop my relationship to God quite
independently of what is going on around me, as if it had nothing
to do with me. If I am to develop and deepen my relationship to
God to be all that it can and should be, I have to be concerned about
justice and injustice wherever it exists within the people of God. I
have to promote justice in the relationships of each of the people of
God to each other, and I have to fight injustice in those relationships
where it exists, *precisely in order to deepen my own relationship to God.*

The Church
When I was growing up, I was led to believe that belonging to the
Church, if not quite guaranteeing salvation, certainly made it a lot
more likely. By belonging to the Church, you had the grace of the
sacraments and the Mass, and these were important aids to
salvation. When parents come to me and confide that they are
worried about their son or daughter 'because they no longer go to
Mass', I wonder is at least part of their concern a fear that their child
has now 'left' the Church and their eternal salvation is at risk. In this
image, the Church is a little like a lifeboat; when the boat sinks, your
chance of being saved is much greater if you are in the lifeboat than
if you are in the sea.

The Gospel seems to say to me that we are saved through our
compassion. It is through reaching out to the Children of God who
are in pain or who are suffering that we are saved, *regardless of
whether we belong to the Church or not.*

Now I see the Church as the reflection of the Kingdom of God on earth. When people want to see what the Kingdom of God, when it comes in its fullness, is like, they ought to be able to look at the Church and get a glimpse of what it will be like, admittedly an imperfect, sinful, human reflection of the Kingdom, but nevertheless a reflection of the Kingdom of God.

So what is the Kingdom of God going to be like? My image of the Kingdom of God is a place where everyone is treated equally, where no-one is marginalised, no-one is made to feel unwanted, no-one is excluded, no-one is treated as a second-class citizen. On the contrary, everyone feels equal, feels wanted, feels valued and cared for. So when people want to get an image of the Kingdom, they ought to be able to look at the community called Church. There they ought to find a place where everyone is equal, everyone is respected and cared for, no-one feels excluded or unwanted.

Sadly, the Church is far from being such an image or reflection. Many, including half the human race, do not feel valued or equal; many do not have an experience of being made to feel wanted or cared for; many continue to feel second-class or uncomfortable within the communities we call Church.

So, if belonging to the Church does not make any difference to our chances of salvation, why then join the Church? Because, in joining the Church, we accept an added responsibility, the responsibility of witnessing to the Kingdom of God in our relationships. We seek, within the community we call Church, to witness, in our relationships with others, to the Kingdom of God in its fullness. We take on the responsibility of ensuring that the community we call Church is a reflection of the Kingdom of God.

The Cross
The most significant event in the life of Jesus was the Cross. Without the death and resurrection of Jesus, his life would not have the significance which it has. The Cross was also clearly, for Jesus as a human being, the most important event of his life.

If the Cross was the most important event in the life of Jesus, then it too should be the most important event in the life of each of the followers of Jesus. So what is the Cross? What was the experience of the Cross for Jesus?

I imagine that Jesus, as he hung on the cross, must have experienced total failure. Everything he had tried to achieve lay in ruins. His life must have seemed to him to be a huge failure. Even the few followers he had gathered around him had fled. He must have wondered where he had gone wrong, what mistakes had led to this. I imagine the Cross to have been for Jesus *the experience of total failure.*

Yet out of this failure, God brought total success. From the Cross, God brought Resurrection. What appeared to human beings as total failure was in God's eyes total success.

In the struggle for justice, in the building of the Kingdom of God, there is often far more failure than success. Our pet project collapses, what we had tried to achieve is destroyed, our life's work sometimes is undone. The experience of the Cross is that what appears to be failure to us human beings may well, in the eyes of God, be success. In fact we don't even know what success and failure mean. I could run the best hostel for homeless children in Ireland; they could all go on to third-level education and get good, permanent, pensionable jobs. People would come to find out how I did it, Government ministers would praise it as an example of their good judgement in funding it. And how would that be achieved? By taking in all the 'nice' homeless children and excluding those who have a drug problem, a personality disorder, who have been abused, beaten and neglected or whose behaviour is appalling. Yet these may be the homeless children who most need help. In the eyes of human beings, I am running a model hostel; in the eyes of God, my hostel may be a failure. Or conversely, I can take in all the most difficult, keep them out of jail, but only for a couple of years, get them off drugs, but only for a while, and everyone looks and says: 'He's wasting his time, all his children are ending up in jail or on drugs'. In the eyes of human beings, what I am doing is a total failure, in the eyes of God, it may be total success. The Cross is the lesson that we don't even know what, in the eyes of God, is failure and what is success. Out of our apparent failures, God brings Resurrection. This is the principle that the building of the Kingdom is founded upon because it is founded on the life of Jesus. God does not ask us to be successful, God asks us to be faithful. If we are faithful and successful, that is wonderful; if we are faithful and fail, that is also wonderful. We have the best of both worlds! If we are faithful to what God is asking of us, we cannot fail.

And so in our building of the Kingdom, in our struggle for justice, we are intensely joyful. We do what God asks of us and we leave success and failure to God. In our struggle for the Kingdom, our achievements may only end in the Cross, but we know that out of that failure the Master Builder is creating the wonder of the Kingdom.

Prayer

Those who are very involved in social justice issues are often accused of not praying, of not having time to pray, of sometimes not even being interested in prayer. They have too many important things to do for God.

However, in the work for justice, there are two kinds of prayer that we cannot easily avoid, that are imposed upon us by the nature of the work. These two kinds of prayer are described in Donal Dorr's book, *The Spirituality of Justice*.

The first kind of prayer is the *prayer of discernment*. In the struggle for justice, there are very few black and whites – there are only shades of grey. It is usually very difficult to decide concretely what to do. I have a young lad standing at the door of my hostel at two o'clock in the morning and he is homeless with a drug problem; do I let him in and risk everyone developing a drug problem, or do I keep him out in which case he has no hope of dealing with his drug problem? And I have thirty seconds to decide! There is no one answer to this dilemma. Sometimes I may let him in, sometimes I may say no, depending on a whole set of circumstances. But it is a very difficult question to decide, 'What concretely does God want of me in this situation?'

Or there may be a demonstration on behalf of the unemployed or some other group in the community and I wish to show my solidarity. But it is organised by a very dubious group, of which the Church and many in society would not approve, and my superior may not approve if a picture of me in this march were to appear in the local paper! Do I march or don't I?

If I am to be true to the struggle for justice, I need to be praying the prayer of discernment. If I lose the prayer of discernment, then the danger increases that my work for justice will become an ideological struggle, or go down a cul-de-sac, that it will become *my* struggle and not the struggle for the Kingdom. 'Lord, what do you want me to do, here and now, in this concrete situation?' A decision has to be made, like all decisions, as best I can, with the knowledge I have, in the circumstances as I understand them. I do not have to wait until I am *certain* that my decision is the right one – in that case, I will be waiting forever! In the spirit of the prayer of discernment, I make the decision I believe God wants me to make. If it is the wrong decision, then if I am open to God, it will become clear, sooner or later, that it was the wrong decision and I can take steps to undo it or reverse it. The prayer of discernment, while it has its moments of formal prayer, is much more a way of being, an attitude, a questioning, an openness. I may not have time to sit down for half-an hour to pray; a decision is needed now. It is this openness, which is the prayer of discernment, which is important. If I have this openness, then wrong decisions will do less harm.

The second form of prayer that those in the struggle for justice are forced into is one that I resonate with even more than the prayer of discernment – it is the *prayer of desperation*. There is so much failure, so many times beating your head against the wall, feeling that you are getting nowhere, or even feeling that things are getting worse not better, that you are forced to pray the prayer of desperation. The prayer of desperation is the acknowledgement that God is God and I am not God. It is the acknowledgement that the Kingdom we are building is God's kingdom, not mine. God knows what God is doing, I certainly don't! When our pet project collapses, when our efforts fail, then we pray the prayer of desperation; otherwise, we become embittered, cynical and angry as we see *our* plans failing.

There are those young people I know who would be doing themselves a favour if they stepped out in front of a bus; their lives are so damaged, they are in so much pain, they are incapable of any long-term relationships, and there is nothing I can do about it; I can feed them, clothe them and help them to feel that someone cares, but their deeper problems are beyond anything I can do.

They will continue to live lonely, pained lives and I cannot change that. Then I pray the prayer of desperation; 'This is your child, God, I hope you know what you are doing because I certainly don't.'

'Pray always,' says St Paul. In the work for justice, praying always is imposed on us by the very work itself.

Sin

In the spirituality I grew up with, sin was 'Doing what I shouldn't do, and not doing what I should do'. It is somewhat of a caricature, but only somewhat, to say that in this understanding of sin, if I made the effort, if I really tried hard enough, I could become sinless. With enough effort, I would do everything I should do, and avoid doing everything I shouldn't do. Sometimes people come to confession and say 'Father, it is four months since my last confession and I can't really think of anything I have done wrong.' I then ask myself what have we been preaching all these years.

In the Pauline notion of sin, sin is something we are trapped into. We are freed from our sin, not by our own efforts, but through the grace of Jesus Christ. The only way to escape from our sin is through seeking forgiveness from God.

The notion of structural sin is therefore closer to the reality of sin as described by Paul. I, who live in the First World, share in the responsibility for what is happening to many in the Third World; I, who am employed, share in the responsibility for those who remain unemployed; I, who am settled, share in the responsibility for the situation of Travellers; I, who have a home, share in the responsibility for those who are homeless. I cannot avoid my participation in this sinful situation and my responsibility for it. I am trapped in my sinfulness and there is nothing I can do to extricate myself from it. Even if I go to live on an uninhabited island off the west coast, I am still caught up in the structures within which I live and therefore I continue to share in the sinfulness of those structures and in the pain which they cause to so many.

How then can I be saved? Not through anything I can do, only through seeking forgiveness, a forgiveness that I know is assured.

Hence the fact that I am trapped in my sinfulness does not depress me; on the contrary, I am not just a sinner, I am a sinner forgiven. And so I can be full of joy, while acknowledging my sinfulness.

Acknowledging my sinfulness does not fill me with guilt; rather it makes me feel more responsible for doing something about the situations of structural sin within which I exist; for doing what little I can for those in the Third World, for travellers, for those who are homeless, or unemployed, or have special needs. Knowing that I am trapped in my sinfulness impels me to work for justice. And to ask, again and again, for forgiveness.

The Parables of the Kingdom

When Jesus talks about the Kingdom, he always talks in parables. 'The Kingdom is like....' The Kingdom is the culmination of everything that Jesus preached; it is the climax of God's whole enterprise. It is the ultimate, decisive event for which human history is a preparation. We might therefore expect Jesus to talk about the coming of the Kingdom in language that describes something dramatic, momentus, awe-inspiring, earth-shattering. On the contrary, we find that when Jesus describes the coming of the Kingdom:

(a) the Kingdom is always something small.
- The Kingdom is like the *mustard seed*, the tiniest of all seeds;
- the Kingdom is like the *pearl* of great price, a tiny pearl; put it in your hand, close your fist and you cannot see it;
- the Kingdom is like the *treasure* hidden in the field, a tiny chest filled with treasures.

(b): the kingdom is always something hidden.
- The Kingdom is like the leaven in the yeast, you can't see it or put your hand in and take it out and look at it, it is *hidden* in the yeast.
- The Kingdom is like the treasure *hidden* in the field.
- The Kingdom is like the seed the farmer sows – he looks out at the field, day after day, and sees nothing happening. If he didn't know better, he would say he had wasted his time. But the farmer knows that the seed is growing under the ground, unseen.

So Jesus describes the coming of the Kingdom as something tiny and something hidden. When I ask, then, where do we find the Kingdom growing here on earth, we look, not for some earth shattering event, but for small projects that no-one knows about, which are trying to improve the quality of life for those who are on the margins. It is the small little efforts, in unheard-of housing estates or isolated rural communities, which are the typical signs of the Kingdom of God. They do not make the front page on the national newspapers, people are not coming from far and abroad to look at this wonderous project. The small little efforts, the little struggles, the community projects which are trying to improve life for those who are poor, isolated and struggling are the typical signs of the coming of the Kingdom.

We can all therefore become involved in building the Kingdom. Wherever we are living, whatever we are working at, there we can help to build the Kingdom. We don't have to wait for a major change in our life circumstances. Each of us can get involved in small little efforts to improve the quality of life and these little efforts are the corner stones on which the Kingdom is being built.

Homeless in Ireland

John is eighteen years old. His father died when he was four. He grew up with his mother who drank heavily as far back as he can remember. Often, everything was grand at home, but he never knew when his mother would come in at midnight, drunk, and tell him to get out of the house and never return. He got so fed up with this coming and going that when he was seventeen he just left. The Health Board provided him with emergency accommodation most nights of the week, and he wandered the streets by day. But on the day of his eighteenth birthday, the Health Board told him that he was no longer their responsibility and he 'celebrated' his birthday sleeping in a doorway. That doorway became his home. He tried to stay in hostels, but it was so difficult to get in – and anyway, he wasn't streetwise enough to survive in them. He finds it safer in the doorway. After three months, he has got used to it. He has a Junior Cert, but living on the streets you can't get a job. They always ask for a phone number or an address. Anyway, when you turn up in old, dirty clothes, you haven't a chance. But the worst was when John got sick. He had gone to sleep on a bright, dry night, but woke up, soaking, with the rain pouring down on him. He couldn't change his clothes, because the few clothes he had were in a plastic bag beside him and they were just as wet as the clothes he was wearing. All day, he had to wear his wet clothes, he had nowhere to dry himself and so he caught the flu. Being sick on the street is no fun. John would have loved to go home, have a hot cup of tea and go to bed. But his bed was a doorway. When he got his dole, he bought some Lemsip, but then realised that he needed hot water. He went into a café and asked for a cup of hot water but they thought he was being smart and threw him out, threatening to call the police if he came back. So he threw the Lemsip away. For two long weeks, he felt more miserable than normal.

To be homeless is to feel *forgotten*. There is no one calling to see how you are, for they don't know *where* you are, even if they wanted to make contact. There are no letters arriving for you, for there is no address to which they can come. You feel abandoned by everyone you once knew – your past fades into an irrelevant history.

To be homeless is to feel *ignored*. John sometimes begs on the street, but everyone passes by without looking at him. John understands. To make eye contact is to create some form of relationship and that makes people feel that they can't just ignore you and pass by. So they pretend you aren't there, and then they don't feel so guilty. But to be ignored as if you didn't exist, that hurts.

To be homeless is to feel *uncared for*. You are just not important enough for anyone to bother caring about your homelessness. Now, if your parents were important, you wouldn't be left on the streets. But they weren't important. You are of no value to anyone. You come to believe that maybe, after all, you are just not worth caring about. To preserve some little dignity is a daily, uphill struggle.

To be homeless is to feel *depersonalised*. You are not a person, like everyone else – you are one of 'the homeless'. You feel like one of those characters in a zombie movie who walk the earth, known as 'the undead', neither alive nor dead, but somewhere in-between. You are a person but not quite a person – instead you are a client, you are a resident, you are a problem.

To be homeless is to feel *rootless*. Almost everyone has a small little piece of Ireland that they can call their own. Even if they are only renting, it is still for the moment, *their* place. To be homeless is to have nowhere you can call yours. To be homeless is to see asylum seekers being given accommodation the moment they set foot on our soil – and then ask, with understandable anger, 'What is wrong with me?' No matter that most homeless people would not tolerate for a moment the living conditions that are offered to asylum seekers. Homeless people are often the first to protest at *anyone* having to live on the street, no matter what their colour or their race is. But your *perception* is that *you* are of so little value, that even when accommodation is available, *you* are not going to be offered it. You find that offensive. You feel yourself getting angry.

To be homeless is to *lose hope*. You see no escape from your homelessness. Several years ago, you could get a private rented flat with help from the welfare officer, but it is now impossible to get a flat unless you have a good job and several references.

To be homeless is to ask yourself *'Why bother to keep going?'* *'What is the point of it all?'* You think that maybe you would be better off dead. Your life has no meaning, no value, no significance. If you were to die, no-one would even notice, you can't think of anyone who would miss you.

To be homeless is to live your life *in the shadows*. In the shadows there is little light, little sun, little warmth. You look out at all those who are busy, rushing here and there, with things to do, people to meet, money to spend; they live in the brightness, where the sun shines and laughter can be heard. But between you and them there is a gulf which prevents you from getting from your side to theirs. And you ask *'Why?'* and no answer is heard.

Disaster Childhoods

Some of the young people with whom I work have had what can only be described as 'disaster childhoods'.

I am thinking of a young child living with his mother who was a drug user. At twelve years of age, he was sent each day into the inner city to buy her daily dose of heroin. When she had difficulty finding a vein to inject, he was asked to help her inject herself. Not surprisingly, by the age of sixteen, that young man was homeless and also using heroin.

I am thinking of a young child who every time he went home, his mother slammed the door in his face and told him to go away, he was not wanted there. He was fourteen years of age at the time. He lived his teenage years, knowing that he was not wanted, even by his own mother and family. Not surprisingly, at twenty years of age, he was found dead from a drug overdose.

I am thinking of a young child who lived with two alcoholic parents. His flat was in darkness as they did not pay the ESB bill. They spent most nights in the pub and returned at twelve or one in the morning. Sometimes, they would have an almighty row, fighting and shouting and screaming at one another, throwing cups at one another that would fly across the room and smash against the wall. The windows would get broken. And the row would go on till maybe three in the morning, when the parents would fall asleep from drink and exhaustion. This child, nine years old, decided he would leave the flat when darkness fell, and stay out until he was sure his parents were fast asleep and all the hassle was over – but that meant staying out on the streets until 3 o'clock in the morning. Not surprisingly, by the age of twelve, he was a seasoned criminal.

The first thing I have learnt from these young homeless people is to be exceedingly grateful to God for what I have received. My prayer now, each day, is a prayer of thanks. God, for me, is the Giver of the Gifts and I am the Receiver of the Gifts. And I have received gifts in abundance and with those gifts came the ultimate gift, the infinite and unconditional love of God. These children have received far fewer gifts, although with these far fewer gifts came also the same infinite and unconditional love of God. When I listen to these children, I begin to appreciate what I have, for so long, taken for granted, namely the many blessings and opportunities which I have received from family and friends and society.

And the second thing I have learnt from them is not to judge. We can never judge anyone, for we do not know what has gone on in their childhood, in their hearts and in their feelings. I know that if I had been born into their family, I would be no different to them and possibly even a lot worse. If I were to judge them, if I were to write them off as robbers, junkies, no-goods, scumbags, then I am judging *myself*, because in their shoes, I would have been no different. As the cliché goes, 'There, but for the grace of God, go I.'

Some of them have lived with me in residential homes for many years. And I have seen the efforts which they have made to change themselves. They have made a far greater effort to change themselves than I ever had to do to change myself. Some of them have not succeeded, despite all their best efforts; some are dead, some are on drugs, some are in prison serving long sentences. But they tried. And it's the effort that counts; it's the effort which God sees. And when the Kingdom of God comes in its fullness, some of these drug-using criminals will have a higher place in that Kingdom than I will have. Because they have tried harder. God's judgement may be very different to our judgements.

Some of these young people take drugs. If I were them, I too would be taking drugs. People sometimes cannot understand why young people take drugs. But what I find hard to understand is why some of these young people do *not* take drugs.

These young people take drugs to hide the pain. Drugs are a painkiller. Morphine is used in hospitals to kill physical pain. It also kills emotional pain. Heroin suppresses the painful memories of their childhood and the painful emotions that come with those memories. I once asked a young man why did he not try to get off heroin. He replied: 'When I stop taking drugs, I feel the pain too much.' When you stop taking heroin, all the painful memories and feelings, which you have suppressed for many years, rise to the surface – with a vengeance. They can overwhelm you with their rawness. One young man, five years on heroin, succeeded in coming off the drug. Several months later, he attended a funeral of a close relative. There in the front seat sat the uncle who had sexually abused him as a child. All his feelings of shame, anger, revulsion came flooding back to him and overwhelmed him with their power. He fled the church. The next day he killed himself.

Children should not have to cope with such childhood experiences. Some children *cannot* cope with them. They take drugs to help them to cope. Of course, they have to pay for their drugs, so they have to rob. Some of these young people have caused enormous suffering to others. They have robbed, they have burgled, they have assaulted, confronted and frightened innocent people. But before they have committed crimes against others, they have had crimes committed against them – beaten up by their fathers, sexually assaulted and neglected. They are both oppressors and oppressed. God sees the nine-year-old child who is being thumped around the bedroom, yet again, by his father, and God's *compassion* is called forth; and God sees the nineteen-year-old who is assaulting others, and God's *judgement* is called forth. But the nine-year-old and the nineteen-year-old are the same person; in our world separated by ten years, but in God's world simultaneously present to God. We are confused – how can we be both compassionate and judgmental at the same time? Perhaps the greatness of God is that God's justice is fulfilled in God's forgiveness. The requirement of judgement finds its expression in forgiveness. We have seen some extraordinary examples of that in the North of Ireland, where people who have lost loved ones in shootings or bombs have expressed their forgiveness of those who have hurt them. They can never forget, not should they. But their need for justice finds its expression in forgiveness. Can the parent be less forgiving than the child whom the parent has created?

And when I reflect on my own life, and my own sinfulness, despite the abundant gifts and infinite love with which the Giver of the Gifts has blessed me, then I too am extremely grateful to God that God's judgement is fulfilled in God's forgiveness.

And there is one more gift which I have received from these young people. *They have made me angry.* The neglect which they have experienced from our society and from its decision-makers has opened my eyes to what is going on in our society. I was blind, blinded by the experience of family which I enjoyed, by the privileged existence where I lived and wanted for nothing, by an educational system which opened opportunities for me, by a job market which could give me a very comfortable quality of life in our society. I knew I was privileged and, yes, I knew that others did not have the home or the education or the job possibilities that I enjoyed. But little did I realise how successfully and willingly our society pushed them to the margins and ensured that they remained there. Many of these young people were trying to climb out of a hole that they were in, a hole that was not of their making. And the support and help which they needed, and which they could reasonably have expected, was simply not given to them. And then we blame them for not climbing out of the hole! This is not the time or the place to analyse budgets, social partnership deals, housing policies that have seen the numbers on the local authority waiting lists rapidly increase at a time of unprecedented prosperity, a doubling in the number of homeless people over the same six years of the Celtic Tiger, inadequate resources for primary school buildings, for people with disabilities, children with special needs... The list goes on and on. Such analysis would, however, confirm what young homeless people reveal so directly and so obscenely – the appalling neglect by our society of those on the margins.

And so I have learnt something else from these young people. I, like many of you, have been a victim of their crimes. But I, as part of this society which has ignored, rejected and marginalised them, I too am like them, both oppressor and oppressed.

Love and anger are two sides of the same coin. You cannot love someone who is suffering unnecessarily without being angry at what is causing that suffering to them. I have learnt to be angry, and if I lose my anger, I will no longer be any use to these homeless young people.

These young people have been rejected, made to feel unwanted, looked down upon, despised. Sometimes people wish they would just go away and stop troubling them. And then I remember that Jesus too was rejected, made to feel unwanted, despised. He was born in a stable because he was not important enough to be given a bed; he died on a cross, a rejected, despised outcast. Some people wished that he would go away and stop troubling them – and succeeded in making it happen. What these young people experience, Jesus experienced it before them. Jesus, like them, lived on the margins. They must have a very special place in his heart.

'For the Almighty has done great things for me'

Ray is a very difficult young boy. He is fourteen years of age, living in a lovely foster home since he was eight. He was never this difficult until about a year ago. He is now drinking heavily, robbing from the foster home and giving his foster father terrible abuse. His foster mother has to lock her bag away and all her jewellery has already disappeared. He is mitching from school on a regular basis and hanging around with the local gang. The neighbours are all complaining about his behaviour. His foster parents don't know what to do with him. They are going to ask his social worker tomorrow to find some other place for him. His behaviour is affecting the younger children in the family, who are frightened of him and his outbursts. He keeps telling his foster father that he doesn't love him, that he only fostered him for the money. The strain on everyone is taking its toll.

Ray has already appeared twice in the Children's Court, for robbing a neighbour's house and smashing the window of a neighbour's car, and the judge has warned him that she will send him away unless he mends his ways. His future looks grim.

Now Ray, when he was a child, was sexually abused by his father over several years until he was taken into care by the Health Board. He now distrusts adults, particularly men, and behaves very aggressively towards them. He has a very poor self image; he doesn't believe that he is loveable or that he is worth caring about. He is hurting very badly inside; and outside he is hurting those who love him and are trying to help him. Unless Ray gets, urgently, the counselling that he needs, he may well end up homeless or in prison. Even if the help and counselling is available, Ray may not be emotionally able to receive it at this time. Ray may go on to lead a criminal career or be involved in serious anti-social activity.

Ray is typical of some young people who have been victims of abuse in early life. The damage that has been done to them may not be evident until their behaviour causes serious problems for those around them and for the wider society. Then the focus may be on the pain which the child is inflicting on *everyone else* by his or her behaviour, rather than on the pain which the *child* is experiencing inside. We may want to get rid of the problem they are causing *us*, rather than the problem that is hurting *him*.

Ray needs to know that he is loved and loveable. But given his behaviour, most people find it very difficult to show him that he is loved and loveable – indeed most people probably find it very difficult to believe that he is, indeed, loveable!

But if most people find it difficult to love Ray, what does God think? Ray was once a little baby in his mother's arms, loved by God and all who saw him. As a child who was sexually abused, he must have had a special place in our compassionate God's heart. And the one thing that doesn't change in this life is God's love. Even though Ray's behaviour has made him unacceptable to those around him, God still loves him with the same infinite and unconditional love that God had for him from the moment he was conceived. What gives Ray his value is not that he behaves nicely towards the rest of us, but that he is loved infinitely by God. Each of us is loved by God, not because we deserve it, not because our behaviour gives us a right to be loved, but because God is compassion. Ray is loved, not because of who *Ray* is, but because of who *God* is. To be loved by God is a *gift*, given freely by God to all whom God has created. This is a gift given to us for life, and into eternal life. This is a gift which no-one can take from us, not even our own behaviour.

Mary is the person who appreciated this gift more than anyone else. She acknowledged her greatness, a greatness which is hers by virtue of the love of God for her.

'Yes, from this day forward all generations will call me
blessed, for the Almighty has done great things for me.'

Mary's acknowledgement of her greatness was not pride, because
she knew that her greatness was a gift given to her by the love of
God.
        'He has looked upon his lowly handmaid.'

Mary, then, is a reminder to Ray that he, too, like her, is
infinitely loveable; that his loveableness, like hers, is not something
he has to earn, is not a gift for the community to bestow or
withhold, but is given to him by the gift of the infinite love of God
for him.

And Ray is a reminder to all of us, a challenge even, as we,
rightfully, seek to protect ourselves from his behaviour, not to
reject him because we find it hard to cope with him, not to judge
him because we find it hard to like him, and not to condemn him
because we find his behaviour unacceptable. For if we reject him,
we reject ourselves, if we judge him, we judge ourselves, and if we
condemn him, we condemn ourselves. For who amongst us
cannot say, 'There, but for the grace of God, go I'. Family, friends,
school, community, opportunities – all those experiences which
shape us to be who we are – are gifts to us from God. Ray is a
reminder to us of the deep gratitude which we owe to God for
who we are. He is a reminder to us, also, that God's love is much
greater than our love.

Just a Ten-year-old
Poor Kid from a
Broken Home

In April 2002, one of the most heart-breaking stories found its way
into the national media. It concerned a ten-year-old boy who was
sleeping rough. The boy was filthy, had untreated scabies, and
wouldn't go to school because the other children laughed at him
as he was smelling. Some nights when he wasn't sleeping on the
street, he stayed with his alcoholic uncle and his uncle's alcoholic
friends. There were concerns about possible sexual abuse.

The boy was summoned, on a Friday, to appear in the
Children's Court for non-attendance at school. His social worker
accompanied him. When the judge enquired where the child was
going to stay over the weekend, his social worker explained that,
because there were no places available, she had been instructed by
the Health Board *not* to take the child into care. The child would
have to continue sleeping rough. The judge – a wonderful, caring
person – requested the child's solicitor to go immediately to the
High Court and get a court order requiring the child to be given
suitable care. The High Court ordered that the child be given
emergency accommodation over the weekend and the case was to
be returned to the High Court on the Monday. On the Monday,
the Health Board informed the High Court that a foster placement
had been found for the boy where he could remain until a
permanent residential place became available.

Good news, bad news. The good news is that the child was
found somewhere safe to live. Accommodation *was* found for the
boy. Possibly, some Health Board official was working until

midnight on the Friday, I don't know; possibly some arms were twisted, possibly some financial incentives were offered, I don't know. But somewhere for the boy to live *was* found, the very same day that the boy went to the High Court.

The bad news is that the *system* had failed. A ten-year-old boy needed somewhere to live; somewhere to live was, eventually, found. But the *system* could not match the two. It required an order from a High Court Judge to get action. Here we had a *system failure*.

Unfortunately, this was not an isolated incident. Each child on the street is a result of a system failure; each child placed in inappropriate accommodation is a result of a system failure. And there are more children on the streets than even before. The *system* is a combination of statutory and voluntary services; the statutory services depend very heavily on the voluntary services for residential and day services for homeless young people and the voluntary services depend on the statutory services for funding, placement of children and training of staff. The system is a complex interaction between the two. However, the Health Boards have the responsibility of ensuring that the system works. A system failure, even if the voluntary services are largely responsible, ought to be investigated and put right by the Health Board.

Sometimes system failures are put right. Imagine if the Health Board auditors had discovered one million euro missing from the accounts. Imagine if someone had defrauded the money, or it had just slipped out of the system over a period of a year or two, without being detected. Another system failure. The system which was meant to prevent the possibility of this happening had failed. But this time there would be an outcry; the media would call it a scandal; questions would be asked in the Dail; outside consultants would be brought in to report on how the system failed; the report would be published to re-assure the public that their taxes were not going to be squandered in the future; maybe some people with responsibility for the system failure would be sacked. Some system failures *are* put right.

But this system failure wasn't one million euro going missing – this was just a ten-year-old poor kid from a broken home.

Unaffordable Housing – A Cancer in our Society

For sale: three-bedroom terraced house in quiet neighbourhood with garden at rear. Price £42,000. Unfortunately, you will have to travel to Manchester to view this home. For sale in Dublin: three-bedroom terraced house in quiet neighbourhood with garden at rear. Price €220,000. And that's a bargain not to be missed!

As one letter to the *Irish Times* put it: 'My daughter who is a nurse cannot buy a dog box and my other daughter who is a national school teacher cannot buy a cat's cradle. In fact the two of them together cannot buy a cardboard box in Dublin'.

Breda O'Brien in the *Irish Times* commented on 'a couple where the wife works in the home caring for four children. The husband earns €54,000 a year but they still cannot afford to buy the relatively modest home they are seeking because lending agencies will only lend them three times his salary. As they have been paying high rents for years, their own savings will not meet the shortfall'.

The inability of many couples, even with very good jobs, to be able to afford their own accommodation has a knock-on effect right down to the poor and the homeless. Many families, even on good incomes, are forced to remain in either private rented accommodation or in Local Authority accommodation. Both these sectors are then clogged up, preventing those who are poor and dependent on them from gaining access to housing. Fifty-five thousand households are on Local Authority waiting lists – five thousand new Local Authority homes per year will barely keep up with the *new* households being added to the waiting lists each year!

This unaffordable housing has many social consequences:

- Emigration: forced emigration, which we thought the Celtic Tiger had eliminated, has returned, not because our young people cannot get jobs, but because they do not see any way of owning their own house in Ireland in any foreseeable future.
- Difficulty in recruiting staff: firms have difficulty in attracting staff to Dublin, in particular, because of the cost of accommodation. Those who do come are demanding higher remuneration to compensate for the cost of accommodation, pushing up inflation and making our economy less competitive.
- Many unemployed people are financially unable to take up low-paid jobs, as they would lose their accommodation subsidies and would become homeless.
- The number of homeless people has doubled in the past five years, almost all of it due to the virtual impossibility now of homeless people accessing affordable accommodation.

But the most serious consequence is the damage, even destruction, of relationships within the family.

Families paying a mortgage or seeking their first home are obliged to have both parents working, not by choice, but by necessity. They often have to work long hours to make up the money, which, combined with long commuting times, reduces considerably the time they have to spend with each other and with their children. The long-term effects of this on their relationship with each other and with their children has still to be researched. However, it does not require a PhD to deduce that the strains within many families will have serious consequences for some families and for society in future years.

And they are the lucky ones! Many families are living in overcrowded households or in expensive, sub-standard, insecure rented accommodation, while they wait years to be given Local Authority accommodation. The strains on relationships between partners, and with in-laws, over time, can become intolerable.

Even further down the scale are those families living in B&B accommodation. The whole family living in one cramped room, with no facilities for cooking meals, often having to leave during the day with nowhere to go. If the B&B is not permanent – and that is the nature of B&Bs – the children's schooling is disrupted every time they are forced to move. If the family is a one-parent family, then the other parent may not be permitted to visit the B&B by the owner, and so whatever relationship exists between the parents is frozen, unable to develop further, and may in fact deteriorate to the point of no return.

And at the bottom of the scale are the homeless, who are now unable to escape from their homelessness into the private rented sector because this sector is in such high demand from those who are working but unable to afford to buy their own home.

Who suffers? Ordinary people, middle-income and poor are the ones who suffer from the excessively high prices being demanded for ordinary houses. Parental separation, deterioration in parent-child relationships, physical and mental health problems arising from the stresses and strains of unaffordable housing are likely to increase even further with serious consequences, not just for the families concerned, but for society.

And who benefits? A small group of builders, whose profits have soared; landowners and developers who have made massive windfall gains; and speculators who have become rich by doing nothing. Some politicians have also become very rich in the process, through their association with builders and speculators, sometimes legally, sometimes corruptly. For most, affordable housing is not a priority issue; it was not even mentioned during the run up to the 2002 election!

To create a society which can give to each person or family an acceptable standard of accommodation, at a price they can afford, and allow them the choice of working at home with the children or working in the marketplace, that is surely not too much to ask for.

But such a project will be opposed by those who have a lot to lose. To achieve it will require a revolution.

A Tale of Two Sisters

The story was bad enough, but the sequel was even worse.

The story

At 1.30 in the morning, a white car reversed at speed down Grafton Street, a pedestrian area. A young girl banged on the boot of the car with her hand, to alert the driver to the danger. A man jumped out of the car, aggressive and enraged. He grabbed hold of the girl, handcuffed her, and pushed her into the back of a nearby van. The girl's sister intervened and was also pushed, shaken violently and thrown forcefully into the van. The first girl claimed that during their journey in the van, a man knelt on her back, grabbed her hair with his hand and banged her head repeatedly against the floor of the van. During all this time, not a word was said. When the van stopped she was pushed out of the door, fell head-first to the ground and landed on her chin. She was not allowed to stand up, but was pulled by her arms, on her knees, through the doorway into a building.

This reads like the opening of a novel about the abduction of two sisters. However, it is a true story involving an unmarked garda car and several gardaí. This incident occurred on 25 April 1998 (the details are taken from the *Irish Times*, 13 July 2002).

A short time after the sisters were taken to the garda station, a number of people who witnessed the incident arrived at the Station to protest. A sergeant apologised to the sisters, told them that they were free to go and that there would be no charges against them.

Unfortunately for the gardaí, the girls were not going to let it rest there. Normally, people arrested and taken to a garda station come from deprived areas, may have previous criminal convictions, and are unlikely to be believed if they do complain. Indeed, not expecting to get justice, they do not normally complain, and expecting, perhaps, to end up back in the garda station at some time in the future, believe that it is not in their best interests to complain!

However, in this case, one of the girls was a freelance fashion designer from Castleknock and her sister was also a fashion designer living in New York. Their allegations could not be so lightly dismissed and, even more importantly, they had the money to sue the Garda Commissioner, the Minister for Justice and the State for assault, battery and wrongful imprisonment. In July 2002, the case was settled out of court and a sum of money, rumoured to be in the region of €30,000 each, was paid in settlement of the case.

The story is shocking enough, but the sequel is even worse. The story tells us what some gardaí *did,* but the sequel tells us how some gardaí *think.* The sequel is far more disturbing.

The sequel

After the sisters had begun proceedings against the gardaí, they were then arrested and charged with being drunk and disorderly on the night in question, assaulting two gardaí and damaging property. Now it sometimes happens that the gardaí release people with the intention of charging them at a later date, but that usually occurs if further evidence has to be obtained or witnesses interviewed. In this case, the only relevant prosecution witnesses were the gardaí involved in the incident and possibly other gardaí on duty in the station that night. There appears to be no good reason for not charging the sisters immediately. On the contrary, the sergeant told them that there would be no charges. No explanation has ever been given as to why the gardaí did not charge them on the night of their arrest. Their case was heard in the District Court in March 1999 and the sisters were found not guilty on each charge. They were left, however, with thousands of pounds in legal costs. However, the sisters subsequently also sued for malicious prosecution, and the gardaí did *not defend* these proceedings. In those High Court proceedings, the gardaí admitted that the two sisters were of 'unblemished character'. The evidence clearly suggests that the sisters were subsequently charged with criminal offences in order to intimidate them, discredit their allegations and to provide the gardaí with an explanation as to how the sisters could have received the cuts and bruises which they bore.

The other appalling aspect of the sequel was that the gardaí, even after the acquittal of the sisters in the District Court, and right up to day before the High Court case, *refused to apologise*. An apology is a recognition that some wrong was done to the sisters. The sisters were offered compensation, but without an apology. They refused this offer. However, the day before the High Court case was due to be heard, the gardaí relented, and in court, through their legal representative, expressed regret at what had happened. The sisters said afterwards: 'We're delighted with the outcome and especially with the apology. But I still don't know why it happened.'

And next?
The Garda Press Office have promised an inquiry to establish 'the full sequence of events'. However, the full sequence of events has already been clearly revealed in two court cases. What is not at all clear is how the garda authorities view such incidents and what actions they will take. The results of this inquiry, as with all internal garda inquiries in the past, will not be available to the sisters or the public. We will never know what the garda authorities think about this incident or what action they will take. But if the sisters had been poor, from a deprived area, and lacking the money and the confidence to take on the gardaí, it is very unlikely that any of this would have come to light. Indeed it is very probable that they would now be serving twelve months for assault.

Gardaí

During the last twenty-five years of working with young people from deprived areas, one thing has remained constant – allegations of assault by gardaí on young people in custody. One of the more serious allegations occurred in June 2000, when a young man was arrested and brought to a garda station where he alleges he was punched, kicked, hit with batons and had his head banged against the wall. All this time his hands were handcuffed behind his back. He alleges that the station sergeant, who is the person with responsibility for ensuring that no such conduct occurs within the station, joined in the assault. He alleges that he was refused a phone call. The young person attended a doctor the following day who noted the bruises on his body and confirmed that they were consistent with baton blows. The young man made a complaint to the Garda Complaints Board, but on investigation, the complaint was not found to be upheld. However, having known the young man for many years, I believed – and still believe – that his version of events was basically true.

Over the past twenty-five years, I have repeatedly heard allegations such as the above. Most young people will not, however, make a complaint to the Garda Complaints Board. There are two reasons for this: first, they believe that to complain will only bring more harassment and the possibility of an even worse hiding; secondly, they do not believe that the Garda Complaints Board can arrive at the truth. As the alleged assaults take place within the confines of a garda station, or in the back of a patrol car, there are obviously no independent witnesses and so the investigation has to decide who to believe: a young man, who has been arrested and may have previous criminal convictions, or several gardaí, held in high standing by society and doing what can be a very difficult job, who swear that nothing irregular took place. In the absence of independent evidence, the gardaí's version of events will almost certainly be believed. Any suggestion to the contrary would immediately bring High Court action by the Garda Representative Association to defend the integrity of its members.

It appears to me that there is a two-fold culture within the Garda Síochána: one is the belief that these little 'gurriers' often deserve what they get, as they are only laughing at the gardaí and the courts who are seen to be too soft; and secondly the culture of silence, where those many gardaí who would never ever consider laying a finger on any suspect, are not going to 'grass' on their colleagues. If they did so, their life within the force would become intolerable.

We have been shocked, over recent years, by evidence of appalling abuse of young people in institutions in the not-so-distant past. This abuse has left enormous scars which may never heal, even in adulthood. The Government has responded to the demands of the Irish people for changes, in the structures, management, standards and protection policies of those institutions and homes which look after young people who are in the care of the State. While the abuse in garda stations is in no way comparable to the abuse which took place in those institutions, either in the extent or the effects of the abuse, there are parallels and lessons to be learnt.

- As in the institutions, a lot of people are aware of what is happening in garda stations (journalists, social workers, community workers, etc), yet feel powerless to do anything.
- As in the institutions, it is young people from deprived areas who are the victims.
- As in the institutions, there is no independent, corroborative evidence available to support the allegations. It is the word of a poor, sometimes criminally involved, young person against adults with authority, power and respectability.

- As in the institutions, few complaints are made as the young people feel that they will not be believed.
- As in the institutions, those who do complain may be treated as liars and troublemakers and fear that they will be further punished for telling lies. In the case of the gardaí, they believe that they will only harass them even more, and give them an even worse beating next time.
- As in the institutions, there are many fine gardaí who would not lay a finger on a young person, but who see what is happening and will not blow the whistle.
- As in the institutions, management will not face up to the problem; denial is the normal response to allegations that are made.
- As in the institutions, systems of accountability are inadequate.
- As in the institutions, systems to prevent further abuse are almost non-existent and what inadequate systems there are, simply do not work.

Within garda stations, the protection system is limited to the garda sergeant doing his/her job responsibly. The vast majority of garda sergeants do so. But if the garda sergeant fails to act responsibly, there is no protection system left, no system of accountability, no adequate system of redress. A proper system to protect the rights of suspects in custody, or young people in institutions, must address the problem of people with responsibility failing to act responsibly. In the case of our institutions, public outrage has led to very considerable improvements; in the case of garda stations, the problem has not yet even been acknowledged.

Heroin – Agony or Ecstasy, or Both?

I once suggested to a young man who had been taking heroin for a long time that perhaps he needed to see a counsellor. 'Why would I need to see a counsellor?' he asked me. 'Well,' I said, 'a counsellor would help you to understand why you take drugs.' He looked at me as if I had two faces and said, 'Understand why I take drugs? Sure, I know why I take drugs, I like them.'

To many of us, a drug user conjures up images of young males sitting in doorways, half-conscious, with a needle sticking out of their arm. The image is hardly very attractive. We may wonder how anyone could possible *want* that.

Yet it is not surprising that most heroin users are young, unemployed, early school-leavers from very deprived communities. Their lives are bleak, boring, even meaningless. They see no future for themselves. They feel miserable almost all the time. Heroin gives them a buzz, makes them feel good about themselves, others and the world for a few hours after smoking or injecting it. Their choice is between feeling miserable *all* the time, or feeling miserable *most* of the time. Of course, within a very short period of time, they are hooked on the drug – they feel trapped. Their lives revolve around getting the money to buy heroin, taking it, coming down off it and then starting again to find the money to buy more of it and so on. At that point, they may come to realise that the price of feeling good for some of the time is to feel even more miserable the rest of the time. But by then it is too late.

Heroin is also an anaesthetic. One young man I knew gave up heroin after many years of using it. He began to feel severe stomach pains. When he went to the hospital, they discovered serious stomach ulcers. He had had them for a long time, but the heroin dulled the pain and he was unaware that he had them. If he had continued using heroin, he could have died, not from the heroin but from the ulcers. Heroin is derived from morphine and morphine is a widely used pain-killer. Indeed, I sometimes hear stories of young people who started to use heroin after becoming addicted to morphine while they were being treated in hospital for a serious illness.

But heroin is not only a physical pain-killer, it is also an *emotional* pain-killer. I asked a young person, who had suffered sexual abuse during his childhood, would he not consider giving up heroin. He replied: 'When I stop taking heroin, I feel the pain too much'. Heroin suppresses the painful emotions which are associated with memories of the past and makes them *appear* to go away. Hence people taking heroin are emotionally immature. Their emotional development stopped at the time at which they began to seriously use heroin. They avoided having to deal with their problems and so they failed to grow emotionally. Heroin can be attractive because your problems appear to go away. But those problems have not gone away, they are still there lurking in the background and have to be dealt with at sometime in the future. This is the problem that arises when someone decides to give up heroin.

It is relatively easy to *give up* heroin; it is very difficult to *stay off* heroin. Giving up heroin using decreasing doses of methadone, a heroin substitute which is a liquid and can therefore be measured accurately, involves a certain amount of will-power and isolation from one's drug-using peers. But the problems arise when one has stopped taking both heroin and methadone. The emotional problems that a person was trying to avoid by taking heroin, come flooding back into memory – all at the same time. This can be an overwhelming experience. Counselling or therapy – both difficult to get – are needed at this point. As many drug users would acknowledge, drugs are not just in your body, they are also in your head. Getting heroin out of your body is easy, getting it out of your head is very difficult, indeed a life-time task. Without counselling, therefore, it is very difficult, almost impossible, to stay off heroin for any length of time.

Strong feelings of boredom are also experienced by drug users who give up drugs, unless they are very fully occupied in some way. When using drugs, your day is very structured – you get up, usually late in the morning or early afternoon, and you have to go out to get your money for your heroin. This may involve robbing, scamming or borrowing. Having got your money, you go and find your supplier to get your drugs. You take the drug and you spend the next few hours under the influence of heroin. When this passes off, you have to start all over again. So your day is very fully occupied; you have a reason to get up in the morning. But when you come off drugs and are not occupied in employment or a course, then the day is one long, empty, unstructured period of time. There is nothing to get up for. Coping with this emptiness is very difficult. The emptiness of each day is filled with all the unpleasant emotional experiences which the heroin blocked out. This combination can be too powerful to cope with.

Many drug users are victims of traumas which they are trying to block out. They then become victims of drugs. They must deal not just with the drugs, but also with the traumas. While some get involved in serious crime to feed their habit, which society rightly condemns, they also need support and professional help, if they are to successfully kick the habit. They get plenty of condemnation, but the support and professional help is often very scarce.

The Prisoner

John, aged twenty-one, was released from prison a week ago last Friday. He had just served an eighteen-month sentence for four burglaries, which he had committed to feed his drug habit. While in prison, he got a detox and more or less stayed off heroin during his sentence. A few times he slipped, when he was depressed and a fellow inmate offered him some heroin and a dirty needle to inject with. He tried to get on to the drug treatment programme in prison, but with over 3,000 prisoners and only twelve places available, he knew he stood little chance. He got no counselling for his drug habit as there were no drug counsellors – indeed, no counsellors at all – in the prison. He tried to see the welfare officer, but with only three welfare officers to 230 prisoners, he wasn't able to do much to help. During his sentence, John got no visits. His family no longer wanted anything to do with him because he had been using drugs. His girlfriend had left him for another fellow.

Last Friday week, John was released. He was looking forward to a new start. He was, for the first time in several years, drug free. It was a good feeling walking out the gate. He had €30 in his pocket, saved from the gratuity he earned while in prison. The rest of his money had been spent during his sentence on cigarettes and batteries for his radio. He left prison with his head high.

But John had nowhere to go. He tried to get into a hostel that Friday night, but they were all full. He slept in a doorway, trying to keep out the rain and the cold. By Saturday night, his money was all gone. He would sign on the dole on Monday when it opened, but it would be a couple of weeks before his first payment would be in the post office for him to collect. On Sunday morning, he got up from his doorway. He was hungry, his clothes were wet and dirty and needed washing. But he had no money. He had no-one to turn to. He was very depressed. He couldn't but help thinking he was better off in prison. He was determined he was not going to go back on drugs. But he needed some money for food and the launderette. He saw a car, with a Pioneer radio, parked on the street. He was tempted. After a bit of hesitation, he broke the window and tried to rip out the radio. A passing garda car saw him and he was arrested.

John appeared in court on Monday morning. The judge threw the book at him. 'You only got out on Friday last, and you're back to your robbing already', he roared at him, 'you'll get no sympathy from this court'. John was back in prison, three meals a day and a warm bed to sleep in.

After being in the 'care' of the State for over a year, John was released from prison with nowhere to live, insufficient money to even last a weekend, no medical card in case he got sick, no treatment for his drug addiction. During his time in prison, he got no counselling, no training, no education. For four hours a day, every day, he had walked around in circles in the prison yard, for two hours he had watched videos, and for the other eighteen hours he lay on his bed in his cell listening to the radio.

Why are we surprised that the recidivist rates are so high?

Irish Prisons

In September 1999, a prisoner in Mountjoy prison was being forcibly moved from one area of the prison to another by prison staff, following a disturbance in the jail. During this move, his jaw was broken on both sides. A prison officer (who was *not* a member of the team that was given the task of moving the prisoner) was charged with assault. The prosecution alleged that the accused, and only the accused, had assaulted the prisoner, for no reason. The defence alleged that the accused was being scapegoated to cover for the assault, which was carried out by the team that was moving the prisoner. The jury did not believe the prosecution and the prison officer was acquitted.

Many Irish institutions have been under scrutiny during the past ten years as a result of incidents which have come to public attention. Incidents of alleged corruption have placed politicians under the spotlight, incidents of child sexual abuse have placed the Church under the spotlight, and various incidents that have caused public disquiet have placed the gardaí under the spotlight. In the case of each of these institutions, however, the spotlight has simply produced a response which can only be characterised as one of silence, inaction or reluctant action, defensiveness, inadequacy or even, sometimes, an apparent cover-up.

One institution which has escaped scrutiny so far has been the prison service. Prison officers have a very difficult job – they are taking care of people who do not wish to be taken care of, people who can be very difficult to handle, who spend months and even years in a confined space, leading to frustrations which they have no way of dealing with. Prison officers have been attacked, they have been held hostage, their homes have been fire-bombed and their families placed in fear. Prison governors are normally people who have proved their ability within the prison service. John Lonergan is the best known of the prison governors and commands the highest respect, not only within the wider community but also amongst the prisoners in his care, for his integrity and compassion. Prison officers and governors do a job which in our society is very necessary, but most of us are glad that it is *someone else* who is doing it and not ourselves.

Notwithstanding, some disturbing things emerged from the trial:

- the injury to the prisoner was not reported to the gardaí (even though the prison officers were claiming that one of their members had, unprovoked, viciously kicked the prisoner twice in the face) until *after* the prisoner's mother went to the gardaí herself, *two days* after the incident occurred.
- The prisoner, after the assault, was left naked and bleeding in the padded cell and no medical attention whatsoever was given to him, even though it was known that his jaw was broken.
- The initial report produced to explain the injury was that the prisoner had barricaded himself in his cell, was brandishing a steel knife, and may have been injured when prison officers charged the cell with shields. It was later admitted that the prisoner was not armed, that the injury did not occur in the cell and that this report was a complete fabrication, invented to cover-up what had happened.
- The prisoner alleged that numerous prison officers had beaten him on the way to the prison van, again while in the prison van, and on being removed from the prison van, was then dropped on the ground, face first.

It seems clear that this assault might never have come to light if the prisoner had not suffered a broken jaw which required hospital treatment, and if his mother had not gone to the gardaí herself. It leaves you wondering what else happens in our prisons that never comes to light.

The jury's verdict suggests that the prisoner's jaw was broken by some one, or others, who have not yet been charged and that it occurred in a way that has not yet been disclosed.

The very nature of prisons makes it necessary that structures are put in place which ensure accountability and transparency. In prisons, the lives of one group of people are totally dominated by another group of people, in total isolation from the outside. The public are not allowed any access and what happens behind the prison walls takes place in complete secrecy. Furthermore, the group whose lives are dominated by others are often despised, reviled and looked down upon by society and it is reasonable to presume that any random group of prison officers share the same range of views and prejudices as exist in the wider society. If a prisoner is assaulted or treated unfairly, there are clearly no independent witnesses, except other prisoners who might be considered to have a vested interest in blaming a prison officer, even if the prison officer was totally blameless. Furthermore, it is extremely difficult for a prisoner to make a complaint against a prison officer, as the same prison officer – or his friends – continues to be in daily contact with the prisoner, in a position of authority, behind closed doors. Furthermore, the prisoner who complains may fear being transferred to another prison at the other end of the country, which makes visits by family and friends – the most important event in a prisoner's week – virtually impossible for reasons of time and expense. And the prisoner may further fear being victimised by being denied access to any privileges or opportunities within the prison.

It is vitally important that what goes on behind closed walls in Irish prisons is made accountable and transparent. Visiting committees are considered, both within and outside the prisons, and even clearly by the Department of Justice, to be a joke. Structures, which promote accountability and transparency, are almost non-existent. What happens to people, sometimes very vulnerable people, who are detained in our prisons, is, and will almost certainly remain, a secret.

The Scandal of All Scandals

There are many vulnerable groups in our society who were bypassed and ignored by the Celtic Tiger as it raced down the road in pursuit of profits and wealth. I think immediately of homeless children and adults, whose numbers have been increasing relentlessly; of drug users who still have to choose between waiting three months to access a drug programme or committing a crime in order to get an immediate detox in prison; of prisoners who seek counselling or therapy and none is available. The list goes on and on.

But the most scandalous story of all was contained in the Simon Community's Annual Review 2000, which noted that 25 per cent of homeless people have been diagnosed as having severe mental health problems (and Simon staff estimate that a further 25 per cent also have severe mental health problems that have been left undiagnosed) and asked whether the homeless services had 'become a dumping ground for the chronically mentally ill'.

Some time ago, I brought a young man to hospital, suffering from delusions. He was diagnosed as paranoid schizophrenic and admitted for about two weeks. He was then discharged and came to stay in one of our hostels where his condition slowly deteriorated. He would not wash or change his clothes, he cut his arms with a knife, he burnt his arms with a lighter and he withdrew into his own private world, talking to himself even in the midst of a crowd. He was re-admitted to the hospital. I wrote a letter explaining that he could not return to our hostel as we did not have the skills or resources to look after someone with a serious psychiatric illness. I was hoping (how naive I was!) that the hospital would try to find a more appropriate place for him to live. The next day, he was discharged and given a note for the Homeless Persons Unit, requesting them to try to find accommodation for him.

I was disgusted. Here was a young man who was totally incapable of living independently, or even of looking after himself properly, who was being dumped on to the streets, where perfectly healthy people have great difficulty in surviving. I didn't blame the hospital – they simply had no supervised accommodation where he could go and live. The sad thing was that while in hospital, with the support and attention of trained staff, he improved immeasurably; on discharge, he began to deteriorate again. Indeed one doctor working in a psychiatric unit for over twenty years told me that he had *never* discharged a patient appropriately. This is not an issue for the homeless services; it is an issue for the psychiatric services. There are many others with mental disabilities who are not homeless, but whose parents, often elderly, are worn out, physically and emotionally, from caring for them without much support, and with no respite care. They know that despite the limitless love and care which they provide, their son or daughter would have a better quality of life in a small residential unit where professional support would be available. They are also worried sick about what will happen to their son or daughter when they die.

There are only two reasons for the absence of a sufficient number of small residential units, where people with mental disabilities can live with professional support, and thereby maintain a reasonable quality of life. The first reason is *money*. Our Government does not consider it important enough to allocate the resources which are needed to give people with mental disabilities an alternative to living on the streets. And the second, deeper, reason has to do with *values*. How we spend our money (both as individuals and as a society) is the best indicator of the value system we *really* live by, as opposed to the value system which we *say* we live by! Our failure to fund those small residential units reveals the lack of any concern or care for the quality of life of those with mental disabilities. Increasingly our society (and evidence is abundantly available from recent budgets to support this) values individuals according to their contribution to the economy, not by the common humanity which we all share. Perhaps it is going too far to suggest that those who are outside the workforce are looked upon as parasites, feeding off the hard work of the rest of us, and therefore not deserving of any consideration. But many in our society certainly feel that that is the way they are being treated.

The whole purpose of an economy is to improve the quality of life of its citizens. It is clear that in our society, where the economy performed spectacularly over several years, the quality of life of many of its citizens has not improved. A report by the United Nations, which measured the extent of 'human poverty', ranked Ireland as sixteenth out of seventeen Western countries. It noted that 23 per cent of the population were functionally illiterate, e.g. could not read a bus timetable, and that we spent proportionately less on health than almost any other EU country. If 'benchmarking' is the buzz word of the moment, maybe we need to benchmark the *quality of life* of all our citizens. And we could start with perhaps the most vulnerable of all our citizens, those whose mental disabilities prevent them from living independently.

A Question of Rights

You want rights? Forget it.

Maybe it was the Child Care Act 1991 that frightened them. The Child Care Act gave homeless children a *legal right* to suitable accommodation. Since then, a succession of children have gone to the High Court demanding suitable accommodation, much to the embarrassment of the Government, and at a cost of many millions of euros in legal fees to the taxpayer. Even worse, The High Court began to question what the Government was doing – or more to the point, what they were *not* doing – in making this right available to children and began to make demands on them. At one stage, Judge Peter Kelly threatened to imprison three Government Ministers for contempt of court, for promising to do one thing and then doing another. He subsequently *ordered* the Government to do what the Government had already promised the Court it would do, which annoyed the Government so much that they appealed this judgement to the Supreme Court. The Supreme Court, to their great relief, decided that Judge Peter Kelly had no authority to order the Government to do anything. All this hassle was brought about by a Government minister who decided that homeless children should have *rights*.

Since then, a number of issues have arisen which clearly suggest that this Government is determined never to make the same mistake again of giving people rights.

The Disability Bill

In 2002, the Government published a Disability Bill which it attempted to fast-track through the Dail. The bill was almost universally opposed by organisations representing people with disabilities, precisely because the bill *failed to confer rights* on people with disabilities. Indeed, sections 47 and 48 of the bill actually prohibited people from going to the courts to seek redress. Faced with a barrage of criticism, the Government had to withdraw the bill.

The Jamie Synnott Case

Jamie Synnott was an autistic child whose parents went to the High Court to try and get a suitable education for their child. The High Court was highly critical of the Government's inaction in providing Jamie with his constitutional right to education and declared that Jamie, and others like him, had a *right to primary education* for as long as he was able to benefit from it. The Government was horrified by this decision and appealed the judgement to the Supreme Court. The Supreme Court, again much to the relief of the Government, overruled the High Court and declared that the right to primary education stopped at the age of eighteen – even though Jamie, at twenty-three, was unable to cope with tasks which would be easily accomplished by young children, and even though he had, in fact, been denied suitable education by the Government when he was in fact under eighteen. Now, once a person reaches eighteen years of age, they have no right to any further education, even if it would improve immeasurably the quality of their life.

Freedom of Information Act

The Freedom of Information Act, in 1998, gave the public *the right to access* a considerable range of documents which reveal the background to decisions of Government or some State bodies. The purpose of the Act was to ensure accountability to the public for what is done in our name and with our money. If decisions are made, and money spent, in the knowledge that the public are entitled to know how and why those decisions were made, then better government is assured. Many of the scandals of earlier years would never have happened if the public had had this right of access to documents, as these scandals depend on a culture of secrecy. However, in 2003, major changes to the Act were introduced which limit what the public has a right to access. It is clear that the intention of the changes was to keep the public out, and avoid embarrassment. Contempt for the public was further shown when the two Government Ministers with responsibility for introducing the changes to the Act decided to enjoy themselves in Cheltenham while the changes were being debated in the Dáil and Seanad.

Ombudsman for Children

The function of an Ombudsman for Children is to take complaints and investigate allegations of the violations of children's rights and to promote their rights. An Ombudsman for Children was promised by the Government *several* years ago. However, when the new Fianna Fáil – Progressive Democrat Government came into office in 1997, it reneged on this promise. In 1998, it was severely criticised for failing to establish this office by the UN review of Ireland's performance in implementing the Convention on the Rights of the Child. Eventually, in 2002, before the general election, legislation to establish the office of Ombudsman for Children was passed. Since then, the setting up of the office has stalled. The Office has still not been established, the post remains unadvertised and vacant. We are now told that it will be April 2004 before any action will be taken. This delay is not due to lack of funding, as funding for the office was included in both the 2002 Budget and the 2003 Budget.

By contrast, the Northern Ireland Assembly passed its legislation to establish a Children's Commissioner (a very similar office to the Ombudsman) *after* the Government here passed the necessary legislation in April 2002. They have already advertised the position and have set in place a process for selecting their Commissioner.

UN Convention on the Rights of People with Disabilities

In February 2002, the United Nations General Assembly began the process of considering proposals for a Treaty on the Rights of

People with Disabilities. Ireland has opposed the drafting of such a Treaty. In preparation for a meeting in June, the European Union has been attempting to present a common position to the United Nations on what the Treaty should contain. Alone of all the EU countries, Ireland is blocking this attempt. Ireland's intransigence seems to be the fear of enforceable socio-economic rights

Minister for Justice's attack on the culture of human rights
The Minister for Justice, Michael McDowell, on 23rd May 2003, launched an attack on the culture of 'human rights speak'. Mr McDowell said that the failed policies of socialism in the last century were now being repackaged in demands for a rights-based society. He questioned the motives of the 'so-called human rights community'. He argued that social and economic rights were more suitably delivered by Government policies than by the courts.

The Minister appears to be arguing that granting social and economic rights is unnecessary and that the Government can be trusted to ensure that the social and economic needs of all our citizens will be met. The Minister was speaking to a gathering of Management Consultants, who probably applauded his speech. Luckily – for him – he was not addressing a gathering of homeless people, or parents of autistic children, or people with disabilities, or people with addictions, or Travellers or people who depend on public health care or children being educated in dilapidated schools, or people in disadvantaged areas with psychiatric problems. *They* know what happens to them when their needs depend, not on rights, but on political favours.

Drugs in Irish Society – Use and Abuse

I have personally found several young people dead from drugs; I have seen at first hand the misery they cause to families, the despair they create for the young people who take them. I have lived with young people who have struggled over months to give up drugs, only to see them return to using heroin again, sometimes within days of finishing their detox.

Drug misuse, while it becomes a serious problem in its own right, is nevertheless only a symptom of a much more serious problem. From the perspective of someone who works with young drug users, day in and day out, I have several difficulties with the way in which the current problem of drug misuse is being handled.

The first is the long waiting list for drug treatment, currently running at nine months or longer for some. There are four hundred heroin users on the waiting list for treatment, but I know many who just don't bother putting their names forward for treatment because nine months may be more than a lifetime for some of them. If you are feeling sufficiently desperate to want to go for treatment, to be told that you might be waiting nine months is just another reason for despair. Drug users live for the present moment – if you are dying sick from withdrawals, you need to get the money and the drugs immediately. So the focus of your life, day after day, is on the next few hours, not nine months. To be asked to adopt a mindset, which looks to a solution to your problem at some indefinite date maybe nine months down the road, is a mental manoeuvre which is too difficult for some drug users to make. Some just don't bother going to the trouble to get their name on the list, others just don't persevere in maintaining contact over that period of time. Others go to jail and on release have to start all over again.

For parents who discover that they have a son or daughter using heroin, their dilemma is whether to allow them to live at home for those nine months, during which time they worry about the effect that their drug taking has on their other children, or whether to put them out until they can access drug treatment. The problem is even more acute in a hostel for homeless young people. The staff in a hostel have the same dilemma as parents, only they may not know the young person as well and the potential for influencing other young people using the hostel is much greater. And so homeless young people are caught in a Catch-22; without a place to live, and support to maintain contact with the drug treatment services, they are unlikely to give up drugs; but until they can give up heroin, they are unlikely to get a place to live.

Some years ago, the former Eastern Health Board promised treatment on demand by the end of the year – that was about 1997 or 1998. Today that promise is still unrealised. I have some sympathy for the Health Services; I appreciate that opposition from local communities has delayed the opening of a number of treatment centres. But a nine month delay is unacceptable and some way of reducing the waiting time is urgently needed.

My second problem is the shortage of residential treatment places. If drug use is, in many cases, related to deep traumas in childhood or inability to cope with emotional pain, then methadone maintenance cannot be the answer to drug misuse. Methadone maintenance is a solution to problems *related* to drug misuse, such as crime, infections and other health problems, but it is, at best, only a temporary step in treating drug misuse itself. To successfully treat the drug problem, then the childhood memories and accompanying emotional pain, which the drugs try to suppress, must be addressed. In many cases, this requires prolonged residential treatment. To be fair, the number of residential places available has doubled in recent years. But to go from about twenty to about forty places, with a heroin using population of over 13,000, is still hopelessly inadequate. Again, the long delay in accessing residential treatment leads many drug users to give up trying, if they have even bothered to seek residential treatment at all. My cynical mind thinks that the cost of providing methadone (€10 or €20 per week) compared with the cost of providing residential treatment (maybe €1,000 per week) may have influenced the decisions that have led to the present imbalance in services!

Finally, the difficulty in accessing a drug counsellor makes it very difficult for some young people to stay off drugs. All those attending for methadone maintenance cannot be seen by a counsellor once a week as there are too few counsellors to provide such a comprehensive service. However, those who have successfully come off drugs find it almost impossible to find a drug counsellor who can take them on. If they are lucky enough to find one, they will probably have to attend a drug clinic to see them – and the last thing they need is to move back into a situation where they are surrounded by drug users.

I know that there are no easy answers to the problem of drug misuse. Few drug users give up drugs and stay off drugs. Their problems are massive and would be very difficult to deal with, even if they did not have the added complication of using drugs. Many attempt to do so many times and fail. But we should not give up trying. A drug treatment service should, in my view, see each drug user as a person that the service is seeking to facilitate to become drug free. Each person on a drug maintenance programme is a person who has been, thus far, *failed* by the drug treatment service. Many drug users themselves see their participation in a methadone maintenance programme as a sign of failure on their part. The drug treatment service needs to set targets for the number of people whom they expect to become drug free in the next six months, or three years or whatever period they are planning for. Failure to reach those targets should mean a review of the services to see where they have failed.

For a society to reduce its sights and settle for a maintenance solution to the problems which drug users face is to fail them as persons and to give up on its own responsibilities to very damaged and sometimes very difficult citizens.

The Crossing of Life

Many theories exist to explain why some people embark on a career of crime. Some theories emphasise personal and family characteristics, some point to social conditions, and some highlight the differing definitions of what constitutes crime that political structures create to protect the interests of the comfortable. All agree, however, that most of those we call criminals begin their career at a very early age and that most of them come from situations of poverty and deprivation. The person who wrote this story is, even as you read it, sitting in a prison cell serving a long sentence. He wrote this, never intending for a moment that anyone else would ever read it. He wrote it to try to explain to himself how he had come to be where he is, how his life had taken the path it took. He gave me permission to use it. He called it *The Crossing of Life*:

> I could see the red van from where I was standing at the end of a row of shops. It was parked at the second last shop. The shop was a sports outlet so I knew the van would be packed with goods. Not only that, but I also watched it for three days. It would be my first time robbing anything and little did I know that it would also be 'the crossing of my life' and that I'd never be the same again. Anyway, the man got out and walked around the back of the van. He opened the big doors and as sure as I was standing there, it was full to the hilt with goods. He

filled his carrier to the top and was going into the shop. I felt the butterflies willing up inside me. I was alert, watching everything that moved. I was like a tiger ready to pounce on its prey. There was no one looking out the shop window. It was the chance I was waiting for. I moved with speed to the doors of the van. There were boxes everywhere so I just grabbed the biggest one. This box and whatever was in it was mine and no one could take it away.

Well I'll tell you a bit about why I wanted that box so much. I was thirteen years old and I was so sick of watching my ma trying to make ends meet. When Christmas came, my friends went to Funderland and discos. We were the poorest family on the street. It's not that I wanted much because I didn't, just the chance to do what every other kid did, but I needed money to do that. My ma could only do what she could do. So this is just a little look into why I wanted that box. At the time, I knew it was wrong, but I was given this world, I didn't make it.

'Hey stop.' I gave a sharp look over my shoulder. The man was coming right for me but I knew he wouldn't stand a chance. He was about thirty or forty and was carrying a nice bit of weight. I was young and fit. I was boxing now for over a year. I took off like a greyhound after a rabbit. The ground went under me at a speed and all that was going around in my head was the things I could do with the money. I jumped over walls and through fields, not looking back. I knew he gave up long ago, but I ran faster just to make sure. I stood at a load of trees and somehow I got the feeling that these trees hid people who were making the same cross-over that I was. I was running in other people's footprints.

Anyway, I opened the box and inside were twelve bike helmets. They were £15 each but I was selling them for £5 each because after all I was selling them to people less well off than everyone else. It's funny, but as I was to learn later in life, poor people have a kind of a code among themselves. Put it this way, if I couldn't stand, there was always a shoulder for me to rest on, if you get my meaning. So, on I went to sell my goods. I got £50 for the lot. And having the money in my hand made me feel something I didn't feel too often in my childhood. It made me feel good.

I looked up to the sky and smiled.

Forgiveness is
the Soul of Justice

John is seven years old. He is lying in hospital with a broken arm, cigarette burn marks on his body and multiple bruising. He has been in hospital several times before, but his father persuaded the doctors that his injuries were caused by a fall. This time, there was no doubt – John was the victim of serious physical assault, over several years, by his father. He was taken into care and his physical suffering was ended. But the trauma of his early years still haunts him. He still has flashbacks and nightmares. He tries to forget, but can't.

Jim is seventeen years old. He has a drug habit which he feeds by robbing. Usually he breaks into people's houses and robs money, jewellery, videos – anything that could be sold for a fix. Most of the time the houses he breaks into are empty at the time – but the trauma for owners, sometimes elderly people, returning home to find their house ransacked, is devastating. Some of them are unable to live there any more. Sometimes, the owner of the house is in when Jim breaks in. Now, Jim has no intention of harming them, but they don't know that. They are petrified when they encounter him on the stairs or in the kitchen. One person had a heart attack.

I have no doubt that John, having suffered so much, must be very close to God's heart; that God is full of compassion for what John has gone through.

I have no doubt, too, that God must be angry at the pain which Jim causes to others, that the God of compassion is pained at their suffering and that God will ensure that, in time, justice will be done.

But the problem for God is that John and Jim *are the same person*. John (alias Jim) at seventeen, takes drugs to suppress the painful memories and feelings of his childhood experiences. He knows no other way of coping but to take drugs. And John must rob to buy them. John, at seven years of age, is a victim of the crimes of others; at seventeen years of age, others are the victims of John's crimes. And there is a very strong case to be made for believing that if John had not suffered at the hands of others when he was a child, others would not now be suffering at his hands. John and Jim, separated by ten years in our world, but simultaneously present to God in God's world, as both victim and oppressor. How can God be both compassionate to John and angry at him at the same time? How can God do justice to John for what he has suffered and yet do justice to his victims at the same time?

We sometimes confuse 'justice' with 'revenge' or 'vengeance'. We want to put things right by making the perpetrator pay for their crimes. Sometimes people are upset if prisons are made more humane, if the courts are seen to be too soft. We want people to suffer for the suffering they have caused us. We want to get our own back on *them* for what they have done to *us*.

But this is certainly not God's understanding of justice. Justice means setting things right. So how does God set things right?

Many people have been inspired by the example of some in Northern Ireland who have lost loved ones to gun or bomb. Despite the suffering which has been imposed on them, they are able to say, publicly, that they forgive those who have caused them such suffering. The evil that has been done to them is overcome, not by vengeance or revenge, but by forgiveness. Gordon Wilson, who lost a daughter in the Enniskillen bombings in 1987, is the most high profile of such saints. Forgiveness of those who have hurt them does not bring their loved ones back, nor take away the pain of loss – nothing, not even vengeance, can do that. For them, judgement is fulfilled in forgiveness. If they, whom God created, can find the fulfilment of justice in forgiveness, then surely the God who created them, also finds the fulfilment of God's justice in forgiveness. The soul of justice is forgiveness.

We have more in common with John than we might think. While many of us have been the victims of the crimes of others, we too are part of a society that has failed so many others, homeless children, children with special needs, Traveller children, poor children requiring counselling, assessment, treatment which is not readily available due to lack of resources and lack of interest – others are the victims of our inaction. We too, like John, are both victims and oppressors. We too, as victims, are close to the compassionate heart of God; we too, as oppressors, are dependent on the greatness of God whose justice is fulfilled in forgiveness.

Joyriders

Night after night, joyriders tear around the estate, the residents terrified, afraid to let their children out to play, lying awake at night listening to the screech of brakes and the cheers of the onlookers, some as young as eight or nine. They have pleaded with the authorities for action to be taken but 'resources are limited, the gardaí can't be everywhere...'

In April 2002, two gardaí were killed by joyriders, fourteen and fifteen years old. The nation was outraged, the politicians promised action, new legislation, tougher sentences. An election was imminent so nine million euro was set aside to build a new detention centre for twenty fourteen and fifteen year olds – a project now abandoned.

But the outrage died down, the promises faded into history. Night after night, joyriders continued to tear around some of Dublin's estates, cheered on by onlookers some as young as eight or nine.

At the time of writing, the nation is once again outraged at the deaths of two more people, one a taxi driver, the other a passenger in the stolen car which crashed into him. Once again the politicians were on every radio and TV show promising action, new legislation, tougher sentences, more detention places. Even if the new detention centre had been completed, the sixteen-year-old boys in this incident would not have been eligible for it (ironically, sixty-five detention places for sixteen and seventeen year olds were demolished to make way for the new twenty-place centre for fourteen and fifteen year olds!). By the time you read this, the outrage and the promises will again be history. Night after night, again, joyriders will continue to tear around, cheered on by eight and nine year olds.

Joyriding has been a problem for at least the last thirty years. In the mid-70s, night after night in the playground in Seán McDermott Street, the grandparents of some of our current joyriders learnt to drive. Even then, the politicians promised action, new legislation, tougher sentences, more detention facilities. And there *was* new legislation; there were tougher sentences, and Trinity House and the Oberstown Centres were born to detain the joyriders. What difference did it make? Thirty years later, the problem is worse than ever. Do we ever learn?

Any attempt to *understand* why kids joyride will be interpreted by some as an attempt to *excuse* them. There is no excuse for joyriding, but there is an explanation. If we want to reduce the incidence of joyriding, we have to understand the explanation.

Two things are, and always have been, very clear:

1. Most joyriders come from identifiable, deprived housing estates, with inadequate facilities and services.
2. Those involved in serious criminal activity, including joyriding, can be identified at a very young age, 6 or 7 years old – some would say 6 or 7 *months* old!

Yet our only response to the problem of joyriding is to lock more of them up for longer. But our threats have no effect on them because they feel that they are already in prison, and always have been in prison, even before any sentence is passed on them. What we threaten to do to them in the future is irrelevant – we forget that these are young people who live for the present because they see no future.

Kids rob because they want money and the things that money can buy. But robbing cars, joyriding and then burning them out brings them no material gain. They risk their own lives and the lives of others for the 'buzz', the adrenalin flow. Joyriding is the ultimate expression of *alienation*. Tougher sentences, new legislation, more detention facilities are irrelevant – these kids are

screaming at us: 'WE DON'T CARE'. And we're not listening.
The louder they shout, the less we seem to hear. 'We don't care if
we go to jail, we don't care if we get injured or killed, we don't
care about you or your cars or your society, WE JUST DON'T
CARE.'

And why do they not care? We have to ask them. 'There's
nothing to do around here. The shops are miles away. We don't
have any community centre here. We've no facilities. None. See
that,' he says, pointing to the gable wall, 'that's our community
centre. That's the only place we can hang out around here. We
come down here every night because we have nowhere else to go.
No wonder we're rallying cars, we have nothing else to do.'
(*Sunday Tribune*, 26 January 2003).

Those involved in joyriding feel that they, and their
communities, have been abandoned. Maybe they don't care about
us, because they have never felt that *we* cared about *them*. As they
look around their bleak estates, maybe they hear *us* say, 'We don't
care'. When they hear us talking about them, in justifiable anger,
as 'thugs', when they hear the politicians promising longer
sentences, more detention places – without more facilities, more
services, more opportunities, better schooling – maybe they hear
us shouting at them 'We don't care – we don't care about you,
about your housing estate, your school, your future.'

And the echo comes back to haunt us: 'We, too, don't care, we
don't care about you or your cars or your city or your future.'

Who is going to start caring first?

Juvenile Crime Revisited

The problem explodes

The 2002 death of two gardaí in a so-called 'joyriding' incident focused political and media attention once again on the problem of juvenile crime – for about five days! For those five days, every TV discussion programme and every radio chat show was debating the issue. How should our society respond to what everyone acknowledged was a horrendous tragedy, the death of two gardaí doing their job, the bereavement of two families, caused by two teenagers who allegedly had been treated softly by the courts on previous occasions? Understandably, in the highly charged emotional context of the killings, there were calls for tougher legislation, longer and mandatory sentences for joyriding, and more detention places. Other voices called for more reflection on the problem, more analysis and more emphasis on prevention. While these two approaches are not mutually exclusive, nevertheless there was in the discussion a tension between the relative importance of both types of response. Before revisiting the arguments, some introductory comments might be useful.

THREAD, a community forum in Darndale, an area of social deprivation in Dublin, asked why 'did two gardaí have to die before society sat up, took notice and began to ask questions?' In Darndale, as in other areas of Dublin, residents 'night after night lie awake to the screech of brakes and exploding petrol tanks of burnt-out cars'.

The situation improves 'when the gardaí initiate programmes like Operation Dóchas or Operation Nightowl. Unfortunately, these initiatives in the community are always short-lived'. 'Why,' they ask, 'is a crisis allowed to develop before anyone takes notice? Why do we have to go from crisis to crisis before anything is done? Why do we have to wait until someone is killed?'

THREAD expresses the frustration of many community groups in deprived areas who feel that problems are ignored as long as they are largely confined to those deprived areas. It is only when the consequences of those problems, which the local community have to live with day after day, affects the wider community that shock and horror are expressed and action is taken.

Some might feel that the community forum in Darndale is exaggerating. However, the total silence on the issue, from politicians and media, after the initial five days of hand wringing and election-style point scoring, only confirms their frustrations. We have moved on to more important matters. Cars still screech around Darndale. The final sentence of their open letter expresses their fears so accurately: 'When condemnation of "joyriding" is no longer the flavour of the month, we will still be left with the same problems and the same danger'.

The Government responds

The Government response – the public demanded a response – was to announce the setting up of twenty detention places for fourteen and fifteen year olds in St Patrick's Institution (St Patrick's Institution is a prison for sixteen to twenty-one year olds). The juvenile detention centres are full, so more places were needed. A doctor, a psychologist, nurses, professional full-time staff were to be recruited. Ten teachers, including a principle, were to be employed, giving a pupil-teacher ratio of two to one. Nine million euro were being set aside to fund these places.

Was this a knee-jerk reaction to assuage the public anger (a general election was very close) or a well thought-out response to a problem that had been seriously reflected upon?

The community in Darndale recognises that 'the problem escalates when particular individuals are "out" … when these people are picked up and put away, the problem recedes'. But this is not to say that they are satisfied with the Government's response. In the light of the Government response, their frustrations are perhaps deepened, certainly justified. They point out: 'It is unbelievable that Darndale has no full-time School Attendance Officer ... that the schools' psychological service cannot guarantee any further assessments before the end of the school year ... that there are insufficient educational supports for our children in school'.

Few people working with children would support the setting up of twenty detention places in St Patrick's Institution, no matter how many teachers and psychologists will be employed – or perhaps *transferred* from places like Darndale. The children will be looked after by prison officers, who will receive some training in child care. There are many excellent prison officers in St Patrick's Institution, who care greatly for those in their charge, but they are not child-care workers and do not wish to become child-care workers. The Social Services Inspectorate is a statutory body whose responsibility it is to inspect residential care facilities for children and to recommend improvements. One of their strongest criticisms is reserved for the use of non-qualified staff to care for these children. For example, in one of their recent reports, 'the staffing arrangements for looking after a teenage boy in an unnamed home came in for severe criticism by the Social Services Inspectorate ... the report found that no steps had been taken to see if the staff were suitable for the work ... the staff were all nurses, mainly psychiatric, and many worked their days off in the special arrangement' (*Irish Times* 4 May 2002). The criticisms were all taken on board by the Health Board and changes implemented. This intolerance for using non-qualified staff and inappropriate accommodation for some children in need of care contrasts sharply with this proposal to care for other children using unqualified staff and hopelessly inappropriate accommodation. The medical profession might call this acceptance of dual standards for children 'Government schizophrenia'.*

Is the response effective?

The Government response is the latest in a series of similar responses, none of which produced any significant reduction in juvenile crime. In the mid-1970s there was an epidemic of joyriding and handbag snatching in Dublin's north inner city. The intersection of Summerhill and Gardiner Street became known as 'Handbag Junction'. The Diamond – a large playground area between Summerhill and Sean McDermott Street – could match Mondello for thrills and spills, most nights of the week. The Government opened Loughan House in County Cavan in 1978 as a prison for juveniles, under the age of 16, to be staffed by prison officers. This was subsequently transferred to a purpose-built unit in Lusk called Trinity House, and the prison staff were replaced by trained care staff. The opening of Loughan House saw juvenile crime fall slightly for the next two years (a person locked up cannot commit crime, except within the prison!). But inexorably, juvenile crime began its ascent once again, the demand for more detention spaces continued to increase, and Oberstown House was subsequently opened on the same site.

But even this did not dampen the problem. In the early 1980s, another epidemic of joyriding occurred (or rather was reported night after night in the media – for communities like Darndale, the problem was ongoing) and the response was to open Spike Island as a prison, specifically intended for joyriders, primarily from Dublin. This was to be Ireland's Alcatraz, instilling fear into those tempted to rob cars. But Alcatraz soon filled up, and the problem abated for a short time. Now, here we are again, debating the same old issue; producing the same old solutions; history repeating itself.

No one disputes that some young people are so out of control, and their criminal activities so serious or so frequent, that they must be detained. No one disputes that society has a right to protect itself. Trinity House and Oberstown were set up to meet that need. The staff are trained to meet that need, the programme is devised for that purpose. But Trinity House and Oberstown are sometimes 40 per cent full with young people who have not committed a crime; they are placed there by the High Court because they are a risk to themselves or to others and there is *no other place* in which they can be safely accommodated. Hence the panic to build twenty spaces in St Patrick's Institution for those who have committed serious crime but cannot get into Trinity House or Oberstown. The failure of the Health Boards to provide sufficient secure accommodation for children who need it, but who have not been arrested for criminal activities, has led to the situation where some young people who are convicted on serious criminal charges cannot be accommodated as all the places for them are full.

The evidence is that providing more and more detention places makes little difference to the safety of the rest of society. Of course, while a person is locked up, society is safe from that person. But the person has, one day, to be released. It is generally accepted that prison is not a positive experience for most prisoners, that if they come out of prison better people than they went in, it is *despite* the system, not *because* of it. If people come out of prison more hardened, more learned in the ways of crime, more embittered, with less self-respect and less hope for the future, then society is *less* safe, not more. Indeed, the media reports on the 'joyriding' incident in which the two gardaí were tragically killed, referred to a gang, to which the alleged 'joyriders' belonged, whose leader had only recently been released from prison. His release allowed the gang to regroup. Society became less safe, not more, as events were to demonstrate.

Two alternative responses
1) The only logical option, for those who wish to respond to juvenile crime with more detention places, is, as Brenda Power in the *Sunday Tribune* suggested (21 April 2002), to detain juveniles for thirty years without possibility of parole! If we took that course of action with all juveniles who commit serious or frequent crime, then society would certainly be a much safer place. The 'more prison spaces' approach to crime can work – but only if you follow it to its logical conclusion! But there are two problems with that option; not insurmountable problems, just financial ones! First it would cost a minimum of €2 million per juvenile. So forget about tax cuts! One could argue, equally logically, that if we were to give such juveniles a cheque for €1 million on condition that they bought a villa in Spain and stayed there, society would be just as safe, but at half the cost. The juveniles might also vote for that one! The second problem is that the detention centres in which they would be accommodated would be uncontrollable.

Why not riot every week if you have nothing to lose? Who would choose to work in such an environment in which their safety or health would be at risk unless the rewards were extraordinarily high?

The other problem with responding primarily with more detention spaces is that, despite their cost, they do nothing to prevent the current five and six year olds becoming the out-of-control fifteen and sixteen year olds in ten years time. Society is standing at the end of a conveyor belt and spending €70,000 per year, per child, to knock those out-of-control youngsters off the conveyor belt and into custody. Would it not make more sense to stand nearer the beginning of the conveyor belt and spend €70,000 per child to prevent them getting to the end of the conveyor belt in the first place?

2) Alternatively, if we wish to reduce the incidence of 'joyriding' and other serious forms of juvenile crime, then we must listen to communities like Darndale and others in our cities. They want *adequate services* for children and families in their areas. What they have are token projects – projects which do great things for their children, but can only touch the lives of a small few. In Ballymun, for example, the Lifestart project has proved its value time and time again. Lifestart is a project where trained persons go regularly to the homes of families with very young children, to support, encourage and help the parents in the difficulties they experience in rearing their children, living on low incomes and in areas with few family supports. Lifestart is working with *forty* families – there are 20,000 people living in Ballymun! A serious commitment to the development of young people in Ballymun, which would undoubtedly reduce the incidence of juvenile crime in fifteen years time, would require one hundred Lifestart projects in Ballymun alone. But the promise that juvenile crime will be reduced in fifteen years time will not elect a Minister for Justice in a few weeks time! Opening twenty more spaces in St Patrick's Institution is far more likely to achieve that. The nine million euro which was allocated to pay for those twenty extra places would fund ninety Lifestart projects over that period of time.

It is clear where our current political priorities lie. But the evidence of history, and a little reflection, would suggest that these priorities will *not* make our society a safer place. We need to invest, not in our prisons, but in our communities.

Thought for the day: Both drink-driving and speeding cause far more deaths and injuries on our roads each year than 'joyriding'. Why is there not a similar, and equally justified, outrage at these illegal activities? Could the reason possibly be that 'joyriding' is something that 'they' do, while drink-driving or speeding is something that *we* might one day find ourselves doing? Surely not.

*   Since this article was written, the special unit for 14-15 year olds has now been designated as a unit for 16-17 year olds. The unit for 16-17 year olds which was intended to be built in Clondalkin has been scrapped (this is the constituency of the Tanaiste!) and under the UN Convention on Rights of the Child, 16 and 17 year olds can no longer be detained with adults.

Reflections on
the New Millennium

As I reflect on the last few years of the last millennium and look ahead to the new millennium, two observations stand out.

First, the extraordinary wealth that some in our world can enjoy: we enjoy a standard of living that is able, not just to satisfy our basic needs of food, shelter and clothes, but to indulge our ever-growing and insatiable desires. But while some of us can choose between fifty TV channels, eat in a variety of high-class restaurants, wear expensive designer clothes and travel on exotic foreign holidays, a majority in our world have to make very basic choices – which of the children to feed today, where to sleep tonight. Many even in our own wealthy countries are excluded from the choices that the rest of us take for granted.

And yet as we look into the new millennium, it is clear that the world cannot continue to sustain the economic activity that creates such extraordinary wealth. The wealth that the world has created is, of its very essence, *exclusive*. It is simply not possible to offer the same standard of living to all our brothers and sisters on the globe. To attempt to do so would smother the world in a blanket of destructive gaseous emissions, destroy the protective layers in our atmosphere, poison our rivers and oceans and use up all the world's non-renewable sources of energy in weeks rather than years. Of course we hope for technological discoveries which might make possible such a sharing of wealth, without serious inconvenience to ourselves, but at this point in time, such hope has no scientific basis. This essential exclusivity of the wealth we have created makes our world unfair and unjust. What is as clear as daylight, so blindingly clear that we often choose not to see it, is that what we now cling to so tenaciously simply cannot continue. If we continue into the new millennium on the same path as that by which we left the old one, then if we do not destroy life on this planet by an ecological disaster, we may destroy what we have created by a series of conflicts, as those who have been excluded rightfully seek a share in the wealth that their world has created.

The second observation that comes to mind is that the world has shrunk incredibly, people have come so much closer together. Journeys that were unthinkable or very hazardous several hundred years ago are now commonplace. We can travel to the far side of the world for a two-day conference or a two-week holiday. And technology has enabled us to see instantaneously what is happening in even the remotest part of the globe and to communicate directly with people in the middle of the desert or the thickest jungle. And we have never been more interdependent. Changes in the interest rates in America have repercussions on the lives of the poorest people in Ireland. A nuclear accident in Chernobyl can destroy the livelihoods of people living thousands of miles away.

And yet, although the world has shrunk so incredibly, we have perhaps never been so far apart. We do not want to get involved in the lives of others, particularly those whom we have excluded. We seek to keep them apart, be they Local Authority tenants, people who are homeless, people with addictions, or people fleeing persecution or poverty in their own countries. We do not allow the poor in Africa access to our markets and we share our surplus with them in a very scrooge-like fashion.

And the distance we seek to keep between us and them is related to the wealth that we enjoy but choose not to share. We see them not as our brothers and sisters in need but as a threat. We fear them. They can rob us of what we enjoy, they can destroy the security that we have built on a foundation of materialism. We have locked ourselves more and more into our own little worlds in order to protect the wealth and security that we have acquired.

The path on which we leave the last years of the second Millennium is a path that will, at best lead to serious, continuous conflict, and at worst to self-destruction. So what direction should we be moving towards?

If we are to share the wealth of our world in a more equitable way with our brothers and sisters, we are clearly going to have to live a radically simpler life-style. The minimum goal that we need to aspire to, both in justice and in self-interest, is to ensure that the primary needs of all are met before we enjoy the pleasures which the consumer society dangles before our eyes.

The spirituality which the Western World needs to hear and to live is the spirituality of letting go. To let go of the desire to have, to have more and more, to have bigger and better and newer, to let go of what appears to us to be our security. To choose instead to desire to give life to those of our brothers and sisters who are dying or living half-alive. And to let go of the desire to have, and instead to desire to give life, and to give life to the fullest, is to be like Jesus, it is to find and embrace God.

Such a radical letting-go frees us to see our brothers and sisters in need, not as a threat, but as a gift. It frees us to reach out and care for those who need our caring. Conversely, to believe in our solidarity with every living human being is the foundation for a spirituality of radical simplicity. That man lying on the street is flesh of my flesh and lives with the same spirit that lives in me. That compels me to look again at the life I enjoy and the death that faces so many others and to choose a radical letting-go.

To live a radically simpler life-style and reach out to those who are in need, is this a possibility, or is it the dream of a naive idealist which like all dreams dissolves as we wake up to reality?

I believe that one of the deepest emotions that nature has given to us is compassion. Who can fail to be deeply moved by the picture of a child dying from hunger or a young man or woman who has lost their limbs to a landmine?

I do not believe that we have become less compassionate – but that we have become more powerless. People frequently ring me up to say that on their way to work they find a young man or woman asleep in the same doorway every morning. They ask me what can they do. And honestly, I don't know what to say. They can of course give a donation to the Simon Community or they can write a letter to the relevant Minister, knowing that the

Minister isn't even going to get to see it. We are just as compassionate as ever, but we no longer know how to channel our compassion and our caring in a way that will make a difference. I believe that the will of the vast majority of Irish people, and people of good will everywhere, is that homelessness should be abolished, people with disabilities should be provided for and the poor at home and abroad should be given all they need to live a proper, dignified life – even if it costs. I do not believe that we want to have more and more while others suffer from having much too little. I believe that we would be willing to make very generous sacrifices if we thought that those sacrifices would be effective. But the social, political and economic structures within which we live do not allow our compassion to find expression in any significant way. We have no way of influencing the political decisions that could channel our compassion to those in need. All the decisions that deeply affect our lives and the lives of others are made by remote ministers in remote departments to whom we have no access.

We need to find new structures of democracy which will allow ordinary people to have a meaningful say. The development of internet and e-mail, if genuinely made accessible to the poor, might soon allow us to have an instant referendum on almost anything, with more than adequate knowledge available to inform our choices. Government ministers could then become what they are supposed to be – the servants of the people, not those who lord it over us.

The future of our planet may depend on finding and electing political leaders who can translate into effective action the feeling of compassion and the desire for solidarity which lie at the deepest level of our being.

What gives me hope? When Jesus talks about the Kingdom of God growing in our midst, he always uses parables and those parables always describe something small and something hidden. 'The mustard seed, the smallest of all the seeds…'

Where then do we find these mustard seeds? We find them in countless small initiatives and movements around the world and in our own country, in small communities who choose to live a radically simple lifestyle, where people, concerned with the direction in which our world is going, are prepared to make very significant sacrifices in their own lifestyles and careers. These mustard seeds are my reason for hoping. Some of these mustard seeds have grown into trees. The trade union movement, a small, sometimes reviled and to many an unwelcome mustard seed, has become an important agent for many small people to share in the wealth which their toil produces; the Green movement, which not so long ago was considered a tiny, insignificant movement of odd-balls and crackpots, has become an important instrument for awareness-raising and even for political change; the movement for the Jubilee year cancellation of debt has brought hundreds of thousands on to the streets to demand a change of heart and a change of policy by the economically developed countries. The commitment of a small number of people, who believed passionately in a just world, has changed our world in a very significant way.

If those living in the year 1000 could not possibly conceive what life would be like in the year 2000, it is even truer to say that those of us living today cannot possibly conceive what life in the year 3000 will be like. What we can say, however, is that without fundamental changes in the economic, social and political structures which govern our lives, long before the year 3000 there may be no life whatsoever left on earth.

Towards a Just Society

During Ireland's Celtic Tiger period of unprecedented economic growth and unparalleled prosperity, the number of homeless people in our country almost doubled. How could this be? We could analysis the effect of prosperity on the price of housing, the demand for private rented accommodation due to the inflow of people seeking work in the expanding economy, the growing number on the Local Authorities housing lists due to the inability of many middle-class people to obtain a mortgage, the difficulty of attracting volunteers to work with the homeless due to the long hours of working and commuting that almost everyone is subjected to, and so on and so on. These technical problems undoubtedly determine the level of homelessness, but to understand how the numbers of homeless could almost double during five years of prosperity, we have to look deeper.

The parable
John lives in a flat on the top floor of a house. Eight o'clock in the morning and he pulls the curtains – the sun shines in. He looks out of the window at the mountains in the distance rolling down to the sea. He sees the ships coming in and out of the harbour and the yachts on the sea. The mountains are sometimes covered in snow, at other times it is a luscious sea of green. The sun shows the scene in all its beauty. He says: 'It is a beautiful day. It is great to be alive'.

However, Jim lives in the basement flat of the same house. Eight o'clock in the morning and he pulls the curtains – nothing happens. The sun cannot get in. He looks out the window and all he sees is the white-washed wall of the outside toilet. He cannot see the mountains, or the sea or the yachts or the sun. He doesn't know what sort of day it is.

Here you have two people, looking out of the same house, at the same time of the day, into the same back garden. But they have two totally different views. There is a view from the top and a view from the bottom. Both views are equally valid – although one is admittedly nicer than the other!

The reality

John is the Managing Director of a large company. He has a good, pensionable salary, with regular bonuses and share options. He works very hard, often having to travel abroad to attend meetings, and frequently working at home until late in the evening. He lives in a fine house in a very fashionable neighbourhood on the south side of Dublin. His children went to the same fee-paying school as he did and are planning to follow in their father's footsteps when they graduate from college. His family are, of course, enrolled in VHI. John takes his family on holiday twice a year.

- If you ask John what he thinks of the structures of Irish society, he would be fulsome in their praise.
- The educational system was very good to him, it gave him an excellent education, allowing him to compete with the best of his international competitors, and it is now doing the same for his children.
- The housing opportunities open to him were excellent; he has a lovely house in a lovely area and when his children are grown-up and have moved out, he can sell the house and buy a nice little bungalow for himself and the wife in another nice little area.
- The job market was very supportive. He had a very good college degree and it was only a matter of choosing which of the jobs he was offered. At some point in the future, he will probably seek a new career or new challenges and with his qualifications and experience, there will be no difficulty in finding a suitably rewarding and satisfying position in another company.

- The health service is excellent, with ready access to the family GP, or to consultants, to in-patient hospital treatment or to surgery.

Jim is unemployed. He had been a manual worker on the docks, but with the growth of technology, he was no longer needed. He was too old now to retrain and there are few manual jobs left for which he could apply. He lives in a flat in a Local Authority complex. His flat is beautiful, but the stairwells and common balconies are covered in grafitti and smell of urine. His neighbours are alcoholics and frequently have fierce drunken rows in the middle of the night which keep them all awake. Drug dealing goes on all day and most of the night and he can see it all happening from his window. He is scared that his children will end up taking drugs. He would love to get out of there but he doesn't have enough points to get a house of his own. His children left school when they were fifteen. They wanted the money they could make in the local supermarket as their father was unable to give them much from his dole money. He couldn't persuade them to stay on in school. They told him that they would never get a decent job as long as they were living in this estate so they may as well take now what they can get.

If you ask Jim what does he think of the structures of Irish society, you will get a very different reply to that of John.

- The educational system taught him to read and write, but otherwise it was of no benefit to him. Few children in his neighbourhood completed second-level education and nobody he knew had ever gone to college.
- The housing system is awful. He is stuck in a flat in which he doesn't want to live but there is a dire shortage of Local Authority accommodation and long waiting lists.
- The job market has collapsed. He hasn't worked for ten years and he has given up hoping that he will one day work again. His children are stuck in dead-end jobs that will not last.
- The health service is appalling. Long waiting times to see his GP, long waiting lists to see consultants or to have non-emergency operations.

Both John and Jim live in the same country, have gone through the same educational system, and competed in the same labour market. But they have two totally different views of Irish society; there is a view from the top and a view from the bottom.

Both views are equally valid. But that is not, in itself, the problem.

Back to the parable
Now imagine that at the back of the house in which John and Jim live is a large garden. It is completely unkempt. The grass is three feet long, the weeds cannot believe their luck (indeed there are probably some new, previously unknown, species of weed growing in the garden!), there is rubbish piled high in the corner and the railings that surround the garden are rusted and broken. Imagine that John, who lives in the top flat, is the owner of the house. John has some money saved from the rental income of the tenants in the house and he is wondering what he will do with it to improve the house. It is perfectly rational to decide that the back garden is such an eye-sore that he will have to do it up. It completely spoils his view from the window. So he cleans up the garden, employs a landscape gardener, replaces the fence, builds a lovely fountain in the middle, plants beautiful flowers in lovely flowerbeds dotted throughout the garden. This investment not only makes it much more attractive to live at the top of the house, but it undoubtedly increases the value of the house. Everyone who visits John complements him on what he has done.

However, the beautifully restored garden is irrelevant to Jim. He has no view of the garden, he doesn't even have a door to give him access to the garden. Jim had suggested to John that he relocate the outside toilet. That would have improved Jim's view of the garden immeasurably. But John did not think that that was a priority. It would have been expensive to do, and anyway the toilet was working perfectly well where it was. He did, it is true, paint the toilet wall. It was now a beautiful sky blue.

John didn't have to live in the basement. He had no idea of how the toilet wall was impacting on the quality of Jim's view. Of course Jim had tried to explain it to John, but John wasn't impressed. Anyway, what did Jim expect for €120 euro a week – a penthouse suite?

Now, John had another thought! Now that the value of the house was increased, he was entitled to increase the rent paid by the tenants. So he announced a 25 per cent increase in rent. But Jim was unable to afford this increase. John told him he had to leave. That was just market reality. John was a businessman, not a social worker. Sentimentality reduces your bank balance like nothing else.

So to Jim in the basement, the very reasonable – reasonable to John, that is – decision that John had taken was, at best, irrelevant, at worst, it led to him becoming homeless. John could never understand those who would criticise his decision to renovate the garden.

Back to reality

How could someone produce a National Health Strategy that was going to cost IR£10 billion over the next ten years, but which failed to increase the eligibility level for medical card holders? If they only understood how people on low incomes are afraid to go their doctor until their health problems reach crisis point, because they cannot afford the expense. But people on low incomes live in a different world to that of the decision-makers. Two worlds, both important, side by side, but light years apart.

The problem was not that John and Jim had different views; the problem arises because all the decisions in our society are made by those with the view from the top – and they have no *feeling* for the views of those at the bottom. They *know* the views of those at the bottom, they have read reports, they have visited the places they live, they have a *concept* of what their views are. But they have no *feel* for those views. There are two different worlds, side by side, but light years apart.

John *knows* that demolishing the toilet wall would improve Jim's view. But the cost is too much, it is too inconvenient, there is little point since the toilet is already working perfectly. To John, Jim is a bit obsessive about the toilet, he is being unreasonable, indeed he is a bit ungrateful. I mean, it's not that John doesn't *care*. Of course he does. If he didn't, he would not have given Jim the flat in the first place. He always makes sure that repairs are done quickly and efficiently. Jim took the flat knowing that the toilet was there. The view from the window is no big deal, says John, not realising that it was the view from *his* window that prompted him to clean up the garden!

The effects of power depend on the *relationship* between the person who has power and the groups who are affected by the use of that power.

Suppose that Jim was a very close friend of John's. John would have had no hesitation in demolishing the toilet. If it was beyond his means, he might have come to some arrangement with Jim to increase the rent to a level Jim could afford and put the extra income into the demolition of the toilet. John's friendship with Jim would have given him not only a *concept* of how much the toilet means to Jim, but also a *feel* for what it means to Jim. And because of his relationship to Jim, he would want to do something about it.

The sort of society we build depends on the decisions that some people make. Those who make the decisions in our society are almost always middle-class, comfortably off and well educated. They understand the culture from which they have come, the view from the top. Decision makers have, inevitably, a stronger affinity with some groups than with others, and so the concerns of those groups will be much more easily understood and felt than the concerns of others. Good people make bad decisions not because of a defect in moral values but because of a defect in vision. Because they are unaware. They are unaware of the problems, feelings and struggles of those at the bottom of society. Hence the priority for decision makers ought to be to reach out, to understand, to befriend, to listen to the views, feelings and concerns of those who are on the margins.

How could a Minister introduce a Bill on Intellectual Disabilities which succeeded in angering and alienating everyone with disabilities and every organisation working with them, if the Minister had a feeling for the difficulties, frustrations and feelings of those who are disabled? No doubt the Minister was thinking of the legal and financial problems which would be created for successive Governments if the Bill gave people with disabilities the rights which they demanded. Two different worlds, both important, intimately connected, but light-years apart.

To build a just society, decision makers have to spend much more time in shelters for the homeless, refuges for battered women, the overcrowded homes of those on the Local Authorities waiting lists, in the drug clinics and on the streets, with mothers of children with special needs, with those dependent on public health services, with those on low incomes unable to qualify for medical cards. Only then will they begin to see the view from the bottom, to feel the feelings of those who have that view. To build a just society, decision makers may have to decide that they just do not have time to open new pubs or motorways.

A decision is made to cut €42m from the overseas aid budget. This decision is made by someone sitting at a computer screen trying to balance figures in different columns. They are insulated from the consequences of their decision. Of course, they understand that 'projects' will not be completed and others will not start up. But they do not hear the cries of street children orphaned by aids, or the mourning of mothers as they bury their children who died from lack of food or lack of medicine. Two different worlds, both important, both interlinked, but light years apart.

The core, then, to creating a more just society in which all groups can participate more equally is to ensure that the view of those from the bottom is firmly and clearly articulated, listened to and respected by those who make the decisions in our society. This rarely happens. No doubt the Minister for Finance, when preparing the budget, will carefully read the submissions from IBEC, the banks and other influential groups. But what happens to the submission from the Ballymun Job Centre? 'Sure what would they know about the economy and the effects of tax cuts on the rate of inflation?' But while they may not have studied economics, the perspective of the Ballymun Job Centre is central to creating a more just society because they have something to offer which no third-level institute can teach, namely what it is like to live at the bottom of society.

The application of theoretical principles will never, on its own, produce a just society. The study of ethics may well produce a body of principles which are the result of rational thought. But the *soul* of ethics is a *sense of solidarity*. Ethical principles may be natural and reasonable – from a certain viewpoint. 'Treat slaves with kindness' may have seemed a lofty ethical principle to slave-owners but I'm not sure that the slaves would have agreed! What appears to be a natural, reasonable thing to do depends on the view that you have. And it is our solidarity with others which challenges that view.

We live in a very divided society, and indeed in a society that is becoming more and more divided. All the decisions in our society are made by those who are on one side. Those on the other side are excluded and marginalised. Their view of Irish society is very different. It does not have any greater *validity* than the view from the top – but it does have *priority*, precisely because it is the view of those who have been excluded. If building a just society depends on the decisions that some people make, then reaching out across the divide to hear, respect and understand how the other side live and feel and think and value and suffer is the essential requisite to building a just society.

Prophets in the Educational System

The bodies in the river

Imagine somebody sitting on a bank of a river on a lovely sunny day, lying there enjoying the peace and quiet, and the sun beating down on them, very contented; suddenly they see a body floating down the river, so what do they do? They jump in, pull the body out, give them the kiss of life, revive them and send them on their way. They are just settling back to enjoy the rest of the day when they see another body floating down the river. So they jump in, pull them out, give them the kiss of life, revive them, and send them on their way. Then a third body and a fourth body, all the bodies keep coming down the river. Well at some stage, they say to themselves: 'I'd better go up river and see where all the bodies are coming from'. So up they go, and they find a bridge where an oil tanker has crashed and spilt all the oil over the bridge. The side of the bridge has been demolished in the crash and everybody walking across the bridge slips on the oil and falls down into the river. So they clean up the oil, put a rope along the side of the bridge and there are no more bodies floating down the river.

The children we are losing

In the last five years there have been 75,000 bodies floating down the educational river. They would consist of 4,000 children a year who leave school with no qualifications, 5,500 children who do not even transfer to second-level education, 8,000 who leave school with only a junior certificate and so forth. What I want to draw attention to is the task of fixing the bridge as well as pulling the victims out of the river. So the first part of this piece is about the need for radical reform of the education system, if we are truly to meet the needs of disaffected and disadvantaged students.

The best of times: the worst of times

It is true that educational projects have been started, lots of projects; money has been thrown at them, but really their effectiveness has been very limited. I'd suggest the reason for that is that if we are truly to meet the needs of these children, the system itself must undergo a radical reform. I have heard politicians describe the Irish education system as the best in Europe. Yet we have 4,000 leaving school with no qualifications, 8,000 leaving school with only a Junior Certificate, 16 per cent who are categorised as educationally disadvantaged and the highest percentage of young people who are functionally illiterate in the EU. I ask myself how can we balance these two views.

I think the different views arise because of different values. At the top end of the educational market, we are turning out lots of young people who are well educated, well qualified, well skilled. For that reason foreign multinational companies are very keen to set up in Ireland in order to use the educated labour force that we produce. If you focus on that top end, you might very well say that we have an educational system better than everyone else.

However, if we look at the other end of the scale, there is something radically wrong with the education system in Ireland. Indeed, even at the top end I wonder how we can say it's the best system in Europe. I cannot believe that the competitiveness of the Irish education system, with its points system and consequent pressures on young people, is healthy for a young person's development. So even at the top end I would question the view that says this is the best education system in Europe. But certainly if we look at the bottom end we would have to say something is radically wrong. I think that one of the primary objectives that I would look for in an education system is to ensure that no young person leaves school without being able to read and write appropriately. If a young person leaves primary school without being able to read and write, that effectively is the end of his/her educational career. To really create an educational system that was geared towards, or open to, disadvantaged students, the primary criteria which I would suggest we need is to ensure that every child can read and write appropriately. If there is a child who leaves school unable to read or write, I would like to see us take it so seriously, be so shocked, that we would nearly want to set up a tribunal of enquiry to find out how this could possibly have happened. Then I think we might have an educational system that we consider to be a good one. If we started our value system at this bottom level of the educational system, I think a lot of questions would have to be asked about the system we are presently operating.

Prophets

Perhaps the children who drop out of school, the children who are very disruptive in school, perhaps they are the modern prophets in the educational system. The prophets in the Old Testament drew attention to certain issues that people didn't want to know about. They challenged the huge gap between the wealthy and the poor, they challenged the kings for not dispensing justice and for being partial in the way in which they made decisions, partial towards their own friends and their own wealthy people. They challenged society to look at issues that society didn't really want to look at, and they got their heads chopped off. Maybe the kids that drop out of school are the kids who are challenging us to look at the system, who are really trying to say to us there is something radically wrong – society doesn't want to know. We no longer chop their heads off, we just suspend or expel them. But maybe they are saying something very important to us and maybe we have our heads in the sand and we just don't want to hear it.

The most unjust structure in our society

I would argue that the educational system is the most unjust structure in our society. Why would I say that? I say it because of the *fundamental role* that the educational system plays today in determining a young person's life-chances. As we are all aware today, it is your success within the educational system that allocates to you your place in Irish society. It allocates to you the

opportunities that will be available to you, the lifestyle and quality
of life that will be given to you.

The educational system has only really taken on that role in the
last twenty-five years or so. When I was going to school, we
drifted through the Leaving Certificate and once you got it, you
drifted into third-level education, provided your parents could pay
for it of course. But the point is that you drifted in – your
achievements within the educational system were not
determining your life or your life prospects. Whether your parents
were rich or poor was far more important. But today it's the
educational system that has that key role.

Therefore if we want a just society, it seems to me that *equality
of educational opportunity* must be one of the key values in the
society we are trying to develop. Every child must have the same
opportunity to benefit from the educational system, to be able to
use it to progress into the wider society and take their place in that
wider society. This requires, I think, two major changes in our
educational system.

Social integration in education
I believe we need an educational system that is socially integrated,
an educational system in which children from all social
backgrounds sit together in the same classroom. If we do not have
such a socially integrated system, then we end up with those who
are better off and more advantaged in society being educated
together and able to use the system to reinforce the advantage that
they already have. Our education system, as it stands at present,
not only does not provide equality of educational opportunity, it
actually reinforces inequality, the inequality that already exists in
society. Now I don't know how you can create socially integrated
education when you have areas where people live that are socially
segregated. But it seems to me that it must be a priority objective
if we seek to have a just educational system.

Fee-paying schools
Here, I would mention fee-paying schools. Fee-paying schools are
not the most important issue in education as they only affect a
very small number of young people. Yet it seems to me that they

are symbolic of the bigger problem within the educational system. Fee-paying schools allow parents who are better off and more advantaged to gain privileged access to the opportunities which society offers to their children. Children who go to fee-paying schools clearly have privileged access to the best jobs and the best opportunities in society. Getting rid of fee-paying schools is not the major issue in the educational system nor would getting rid of them make a huge difference to the educational system. But they are symptomatic of the problem.

How do we get the decision makers in our society to look at the inequality that fee-paying schools promote within the educational system. Their own children are probably going to fee-paying schools; their friends and social acquaintances are sending their children to fee-paying schools; and voters who have considerable influence and standing in society are sending their children to fee-paying schools. Therefore it is very difficult to get a situation where the issue of fee-paying schools would be up for question and under criticism. Every parent wants the best for their children and if they can afford to pay for the benefits that fee-paying schools provide, then many will. Those who are currently benefiting from the education system will resist any fundamental change to the system, which would give disadvantaged children a better opportunity. And because those who benefit from the system are those who are better off, more influential, better connected and who vote, it is difficult to bring about change to the benefit of disadvantaged children.

So the first change in the educational system that I believe we ought to seek is to have a socially integrated system, a system which does not allow those who are better off to use their wealth and position to give their children a privileged education and privileged access, subsequently, to Irish society.

A just education system has to be comprehensive

The second change that I think we need is a *more comprehensive education*. The present academic education is clearly to the benefit of a group in our society who are already advantaged. A move towards a more comprehensive style of education where manual skills, skills that are not just academic, are also part of the assessment would be to balance out the curriculum so that those that are disadvantaged can be on a more level playing field. Young working class people say to me 'What is the point in learning all the mountain ranges in Russia? What an earth has that got to do with me getting a job'. They would be far more interested in learning motor mechanics, or a bit of carpentry, or working with metals than they would be in more academic subjects. We also need a new form of assessment. Putting everything into one exam over a week or two weeks at the end of a six-year education seems to me, not just an enormous and unhelpful pressure, but undesirable from many points of view. A modular system would, I think, be very helpful to disadvantaged children. I would also fully support the whole notion of educational credits for those who left school without adequate qualifications and that would be available to them to be used at any point in the future if they chose to continue their education.

What about the kids who are there now?
So I think those who are working primarily in direct relationship with disadvantaged and disaffected children need to promote radical structural change within the educational system. They need to belong to the ERA, the Educational Reform Association, if we are to truly meet the needs of those disaffected children we are working with. We need reform of the educational system itself. It's not enough to add an extra programme here, to put extra money in there, to have extra teachers; that's good, it makes some difference, but that will not fundamentally alter the situation of disadvantaged and disaffected children within the educational system.

Secondly, not only have we got to go up and fix the bridge, we have to pull the bodies out of the river. So while we are waiting for the reforms to be carried out (and we may be waiting for a long time!), we still have to deal with the kids who are there. If a kid knocks on my door at two o'clock in the morning and says he has left home, it's no use my saying to him that I am lobbying the Minister and doing every thing possible, and that in five years time there will be a perfect system and he won't have to worry. We have to deal with the kids who are currently there. At this point, because I'm not involved in the educational system, I want to talk about working with the young people that we have in our hostel. But many of the points would, I imagine, carry over pretty directly into working with difficult young people in school.

Our attitude towards difficult young people

I taught for two years, thirty years ago, and gave it up as a bad job. So I have the height of respect for teachers. But it's not for me to tell them how to work with disadvantaged children. I can only talk about the children that come to us, who would have been, a year or two earlier, amongst the disaffected students in their schools.

The first challenge they present to me is to look at my attitude to these children. These children can be very difficult, very disruptive, very problematic, as teachers very well know. There is a basic attitude that we have to examine ourselves on. Why are they being difficult and disruptive? We can either say they are little brats (and there's that part of us that wants to say they are little brats, when they are being difficult and problematic and wearing us down), or we can say that they behave this way because their fundamental needs have not been met. Their needs have not been met by their families, their needs have not been met in the community, and their needs have not been met within their peer groups. It is because those needs have not, and are not being, met that they are acting out, and they are behaving the way they are. So my fundamental attitude towards the young people in that situation would be to see them as victims, and not as the cause of their own problems. Therefore, without necessarily being soft, I see them as people who desperately need some sort of support and help.

The importance of self-esteem

The first glaring characteristic of the young people we would be dealing with is an enormous lack of self-esteem. They all feel bad about themselves, they feel they are failures, that they are no good, that they are rejects. I remember one young lad, who lived in our hostel for quite a long time, and was then serving a prison sentence. He wrote to me from prison and he said in the letter, 'Well, Peter, one thing I have learnt from you is that I am not such a bad person after all'. I think that maybe that's as much as we can achieve with some of the young people we are dealing with. Now if you are teaching religion to a kid who has no self-esteem you are on a loser straight away.

You can't talk about God to a young person who has no self-esteem. It just doesn't make sense, it depresses them. So giving a person back their self-esteem, giving a person some sense of self-respect and of their own dignity is the core of what we are trying to do. If we don't do that, we can feed them, clothe them, look after them, but we are wasting our time. Part of giving them self-esteem is that *we* have to believe that they can succeed. And that's very difficult with some of the young people we have to deal with. It can be very difficult to really convince yourself, yes, they can get a job and hold it, yes, they can do OK in society, yes, they can hold down a relationship with a girlfriend or a boyfriend. But if *I* don't believe they can do it, there isn't a hope of *them* believing they can do it. So we have to communicate to those young people who see themselves as failures and dropouts the belief that they can do it. So the most important thing that we have to achieve in our hostels is to try and give back to these young people a sense of their self-respect.

A personal relationship
In order to give a young person back their self-respect, you actually have to *like* them. That can be very difficult at times! And to like them you have to get close to them. There has to be some sort of personal relationship, and it's the personal relationship that changes them. It's knowing that they have somebody that understands them, that likes them, is concerned about them, cares for them; that's what these children need.

Now, there is a balance needed here. It is important that the staff in our hostels keep their own personal space, which excludes the young people they care for. Obviously, staff cannot treat one child differently from the others, nor can they give the impression of doing so. Yet the relationship must go beyond the purely professional, if we are really to give these children back their sense of being important, being worth caring for, being loveable.

Consistency

The second thing I would say in relation to the young people in our hostels is that the most important thing they need is consistency – a consistency of approach by all the staff. But it's extraordinarily difficult to have a consistency of approach. First you need a policy about how you are going to deal with these particular young people. A school has to have a policy, and that policy must be bought into by all the staff and has to be adhered to by all the staff. That's difficult because staff have different personalities and would relate to these difficult young people in different ways. Staff will relate differently at the end of a tiring day than they do at the beginning of the day. So it's difficult to maintain consistency. Yet I think the most significant thing in the lives of these young people that will make a difference is that there is that consistency from all those who are working with them.

The question of exclusion

In our own hostels every effort is made not to have to exclude young people. One hostel, for twelve to sixteen year olds, in which I am involved, has, in the last twenty years, only ever thrown out one young person. That young person was a very serious risk, not just to his health, but even to the lives of the other children in the hostel. The staff made every effort to work with him, gave him personal attention as often as they could, kept a close supervisory eye on him, but at the end of a long time trying, it was decided that the risk to the other children was too much. But the policy was that you had to have a special board meeting to take such a decision. This couldn't be a decision that could be made at an ordinary board meeting and squeezed into ten minutes during the course of other business! A special board meeting had to be held. The first item on the agenda was the reasons why this kid should stay in the hostel. Only after that was there a discussion as to why he should not stay in the hostel. Then a decision was taken, in this case a decision that it was impossible to reasonably guarantee the safety of the other young residents. But the policy to work with difficult young people as long as possible meant that a decision to exclude a child was such a major one that it could not be made during the course of ordinary business

Now I fully appreciate that schools have to exclude some pupils. Some pupils have problems with the school or psychiatric problems or psychological problems that schools simply cannot cope with, schools often with limited resources. But I think a policy that makes it very difficult for a child to be suspended or expelled needs to be in place.

Standards that defy the law of gravity

Another thing we have tried to implement in our hostels is, what I would call, 'defying the law of gravity'. There is a tendency in a hostel, or indeed any institution, for the standards, which are demanded, to keep rising up and up. Suppose you have six kids in a hostel and one of them is particularly difficult. We all like to have an easy life and we all like to have fewer problems rather than more problems. So there is a natural tendency to say that if this kid wasn't in the hostel, life for the other kids (the staff couldn't possibly be thinking of themselves, of course!) would be so much easier and their development would be so much better. Since it would be so much better for the other kids if this particular child weren't in the hostel, there is a pressure, which may be sub-conscious, to either arrange for the child to leave or be thrown out. But the problem then arises that once you've thrown that child out, there will be another child who is perceived as making life difficult. And it may well be that this second child could be one of the original five who wasn't previously perceived as being a problem. There is always the *one* child who is perceived as being more difficult. And human nature being what it is, we would all like a quieter life if we can get it. That can be achieved by getting rid of this child, but we don't say it quite as bluntly as that. No, for the sake of the other children in the hostel, we have got to get rid of this one! So there is this raising of standards all the time, it's a natural tendency we've got to resist. Part of the resistance is to have in place a policy that makes it very difficult to throw somebody out. So we have to look at our own prejudices and our own self-interest when we are relating to these very difficult kids. The decisions we are making – are we making them for reasons of our own convenience and our own self interest, or are we making them in the interests of the children themselves?

I think it's very important that those working with disadvantaged young people directly in a school are seen as representing all the staff in the school. Perhaps I would compare them with the role of community gardaí in the neighbourhood. Many of the young people I am talking about see the gardaí as people who hassle them, who arrest them, who abuse them verbally and maybe even bash them up now and again. But in many neighbourhoods now, you'll have one or two community gardaí whose job is to work with the community, get on with people and to be nice to people. These young people see this split between the rest of the gardaí and the community gardaí. The community gardaí will stop them on the street, talk to them, be nice to them and ask them how they are getting on, while the other gardaí will continue to hassle them and bash them up now and again. It's very important that we don't have this split amongst the staff, where one or two are assigned to work with these young people while the rest of the school carries on simply as before.

Not shutting the door
In our hostel we have a policy of not shutting the door on anybody, even if we have to put them out or suspend them. We would never say to anyone, 'you are gone now, we don't want to see you back'. If someone, for whatever reason has to be put out, for example, if they had a serious drug problem and were not willing to address it, or if they were dealing in drugs, we would never say, 'we don't want to see you again'. We would always say 'you have to leave, but if circumstances change, you are welcome to come back', and so the door remains open. Otherwise their self-esteem and self-respect and self-dignity take another dive. What we are trying to say to them is 'look, we really are willing to work with you, we are certainly prepared to care for you, but your circumstances have to change. If they change we are more than willing to do that'. It's important that we don't shut the door on young people as if it was a final act, because that simply reinforces the lack of self-respect, and the low self-image they have.

Looking at the long-term
In our hostels you are always looking towards the long term. You take a child in, say, at sixteen years of age, for maybe three or four

years, but the fruits of the work you do may not really be apparent
until they are in their mid-twenties. They may go through very
difficult stages. While they are in the hostel they may go through
problems with drugs, may go through problems with the law, may
have enormous apathy and be unwilling to work. You may not see
great results in the short term but the work that you do with
them, the building of self-confidence, the consistency of
approach, may only bear fruit when those young people have left
school a number of years, as they mature and grow older. Only
then may the benefits of what you have being doing become
visible to you and apparent in their lives.

Why was Jesus Executed?

Some societies execute people who have either committed some exceptionally serious crime or who are considered a threat to the well-being of the society or to its leadership. Why was Jesus executed? Because the God that Jesus revealed was, indeed, a serious threat.

Listen to your feelings as you read the following story:

> John is forty years old and a wonderful father to his children and a faithful husband to his wife. He works very hard to support his family. He goes to church every Sunday and the children go with him. He tries to live a good life and keep the commandments. He is involved in the local community, visiting the sick and the elderly.
>
> Joe is also forty years old. He has been an alcoholic since his teen years. The neighbours often have to give refuge to his wife, when, in a drunken rage, he decides to beat her up. Some weeks he drinks all his dole money and his children have to go hungry or depend on the Vincent de Paul. His children are terrified of him and are receiving counselling. He hasn't been to church for years.
>
> Both John and Joe died and went up before God for the final judgement. Joe was taken into heaven before John and was given a higher place in the Kingdom of God than John.

What is your reaction? My own reaction is to feel that what God has done is very unfair, very unjust. Why should John have bothered trying to live a good life? Why didn't he just go boozing like Joe? I feel resentful that God could do this to John. I feel angry that Joe should somehow be rewarded by God. Perhaps I feel that if God is like that, you can keep him! Which actually is why Jesus was executed, as I will try to explain.

There are two problems with my very natural reaction:

1. I am *judging* Joe. I am judging that he does not deserve to receive this from God. But in fact, I have no idea of why Joe lived the way he lived. I have no idea of what went on in his childhood, in his heart, in his feelings, in his life. Maybe Joe suffered appalling sexual abuse or violence in his childhood and his drinking was his only way of shutting out the pain. Maybe... maybe... I just don't know. Therefore I cannot judge. But God knows. Maybe Joe, because of childhood suffering, has a very special place in the heart of the God of compassion. As Jesus always insisted: 'Do not judge and you will not be judged'.

2. The second problem is the implication – never of course explicitly stated – that somehow we can *earn* the kingdom of God, that some of us *deserve* it more than others. Trying to live a good life gives us some *right* to the Kingdom of God. However, none of us deserves the Kingdom of God. The Kingdom of God is God's gift, to give freely to whomever God chooses. We have no right to complain at God's choices. John, like Joe, will only enter the Kingdom of God through God's forgiveness.

The God that John – and I – am comfortable with is the *God of righteousness*, a God who rewards the good (as defined by ourselves) and punishes the wicked (as defined by ourselves), because than we know where we stand with God. We have God sussed. And John – and I – (while of course acknowledging ourselves as unworthy sinners!) actually do quite well out of this way of reckoning, unlike poor Joe, who is for the chop.

But Jesus came to tell us who our God *really* is. And the God that Jesus revealed is a *God of compassion*, a God who loves us so much that not even our imagination can grasp the extent of God's love.

But then why was Jesus executed? You don't execute someone who tells you that you are loved! The sting in the tail of Jesus' revelation was that not only am *I* loved by God, but *everyone else* is also loved by God. And *that* has radical implications for the way we live our lives.

Jesus talked about the compassion and love of God for the prostitutes, the tax collectors, the woman taken in adultery, the infirm, the poor, and insisted that their dignity as beloved children of God be recognised and affirmed. But these were groups whom the Jewish authorities of his time despised and taught others to despise, whom they cast out and taught others to cast out, whom they rejected and taught others to reject – all in the name of a God of righteousness. Jesus' revelation of who God is had implications, not just for the values which each individual Jew held and for the way in which they lived their lives, but for the social, political and cultural expression of those values in the life of the society in which they lived.

The Jewish authorities, then, saw Jesus, and the God whom he revealed, as someone who demanded radical change. He was therefore a threat to the faith and values of the Jewish people, someone who was leading them astray, who was undermining their traditions. And they were right. The God that Jesus revealed was indeed a threat to the established way of life. If God was in fact a God of compassion, who loved others as much as myself, then fundamental changes in the way that people lived were required. Jesus had to be got rid of.

And if Jesus returned to earth today, he would again have to be got rid of. Most of us actually cannot afford to believe in a God of compassion. Only sinners, and those humble enough not to judge others, can dare to believe in a God of compassion. To believe in a God who not only loves me but who also loves those that are starving, are homeless, are addicted, are abusing, are robbing, are dealing in drugs, who loves the neighbour I cannot stand, who loves those I disagree with, has radical implications for our behaviour and our way of life, implications that we would prefer not to contemplate. By getting rid of Jesus, we can return to loving a God with whom we, without changing, are comfortable, but a God who does not exist!

Our Notion of Sin

Imagine a man sitting by the side of a lake, on a lovely sunny day, enjoying the peace and quiet. Beside him, a child is paddling in the lake. Now the child takes one step too far and is out of his depth. He is screaming for help and splashing the water, crying out for someone to help him. Now, what would the parents of that child think if the man at the side of the lake did absolutely nothing to try and save the child and the child were to drown? The parents would be so angry, they would find it very difficult to forgive the man. If the man had broken into their house, tied them up, robbed them, taken off in the family car, crashed it and burnt it out – the parents would find all that easier to forgive, than to forgive him for what he failed to do at the side of the lake.

When I was growing up, we were taught that sin was any act or omission that was contrary to the law of God. In other words, sin was defined by reference to the law. Since the law was clear, you knew exactly where you stood with God. When you went to confession, you racked your brains to think of all those acts you did which were forbidden and those you failed to do which were commanded.

I now have a different understanding of sin. The effect of sin is to cause suffering or harm to another human being (or to myself, and hence ultimately to another). For me, sin is my complicity in the suffering of others. There are two ways in which I am complicit in their suffering.

Like the man at the side of the lake , I understand sin now as my failure to reach out to the sufferings of others, to try and relieve that suffering.

God is our parent. And God is passionately concerned with the suffering of God's children. When we just couldn't be bothered to reach out to one of God's children and take some of the pain from their shoulders, that is the sin that God finds hardest to forgive. 'Depart from me you cursed, into everlasting flames, prepared for the devil and his angels. For I was hungry and you did nothing, I was thirsty and you did nothing, I was a stranger and you did nothing…'

Each day, I fail to reach out, I fail often even to notice the suffering of others. My failure to reach out and remove some of the suffering means that the suffering of others continues. And thereby I am responsible and complicit in their suffering. That is my sinfulness.

Secondly, I am complicit in the suffering of others through my participation in the structures which cause pain to others. The poverty of the developing world is due, in part, to the failure of the Western, economically-developed, nations to open their markets to the exports of those countries, to pay a just price for their commodities, to relieve the unpayable debt they owe. I am part of this structure, even if I do not wish to be the cause of their suffering. I therefore share some responsibility for the poverty and suffering which we impose on developing nations. Similarily, I am part of a society that allows homeless children and adults to sleep on the street. I may not want that to happen, I may even be working to help homeless people, but by being part of that society that denies to them a place to live, I share in the responsibility for their suffering. Every time I drink a cup of coffee, every time I buy a litre of petrol, every time I take the car out of the garage, I am part of a society that is oppressing others. That too is my sinfulness.

A mother once came to me and said: 'Father, I don't know what to do about my son. He has been using drugs for the past seven years. He has robbed everything from my home, my money, jewellery, the video. He has sometimes asked me for money for drugs when he was dying sick and if I didn't have it, he would smash up the house, all the windows, the TV. And sometimes he would even hit me. I just don't know what to do with him anymore.' 'Where is he now?' I asked her. 'He's in jail, Father, and it's the first bit of peace I have had in seven years.' 'And do you go to visit him?' I asked. 'Father, every Saturday afternoon, without fail, I go up to visit him. Sure, isn't he still my son.'

For me that was an image of unconditional love – 'Sure isn't he still my son'. If that mother could love her son after all that he had done, then God's love is no less, indeed infinitely more.

I am a sinner and trapped in my sinfulness. This does not depress or demoralise me. I am a sinner, but I am a sinner who is constantly being forgiven. I know that I am forgiven because, God, like the mother in the story, loves me unconditionally.

The forgiveness of God frees me from my sinfulness. Being conscious of my sinfulness does not impose on me a useless and demoralising guilt, rather it makes me feel more responsible. It pushes me to see how I can respond more adequately to the suffering of others, to do what little I can, in the knowledge that the little I can do is of infinite value to others and to God. 'Even a cup of water given to one of these little ones will not lose its reward'.

Liberation and Development

Jesus and the marginalised

When I look at the life of Jesus, I find three groups to whom he reached out in a preferential way:

1. The sick, the lame, the blind, the deaf, the dumb – those who are afflicted with some infirmity.
2. The poor – what today we would call the ordinary person in the street, the little person of no importance, with no clout.
3. Public sinners, e.g. tax-collectors and prostitutes.

What have these three groups got in common? What they have in common is the attitude of society towards them and the way they are treated by the society in which they live. They were all despised, looked down upon, treated as second-class citizens, not wanted, kept at arm's length. They shared this attitude for different reasons.

The infirm were looked down upon because it was believed that they had committed some sin and were being punished by God.

Similarly, the poor were despised because they didn't keep the Law. They didn't keep the Law because they didn't know the Law. The Law, by the time of Jesus, had become so complicated, consisting of thousands of minute prescriptions governing every aspect of everyday life, that in order to know the Law you had to study the Law. To study the Law, you had to have the education and money to do so. The poor had neither and so could not know the Law or keep the Law in all its detail.

And public sinners were despised because of their occupation. The groups that Jesus preferentially reached out to had in common that they were all marginalised in the society to which they belonged. The attitudes of society towards them and the way society treated them ensured that they were kept apart, at arms length.

Dignity

And why did Jesus reach out to these groups preferentially? It seems to me that it has to do with *dignity*. One way of summing up the Gospel is to say that, as God is the parent of us all, each of us has the same dignity of being a child of God, no matter who we are or what we may have done. When Jesus comes and finds some whose dignity is being undermined or denied by the attitudes of society and the way in which they are treated, then he must respond, if he is to be true to the revelation of God which he came to bring. And he responds in three different ways:

1. He affirms their dignity by the way in which he himself relates to them. By reaching out to them in a respectful and dignified way, he communicates to them a sense of their own dignity, in the face of the contrary message which they continually receive from society.
2. He challenges the attitudes of that society which look down upon such people and he challenges the structures which keep them in their marginalised place. Thus he defends the woman who washes his feet and dries them with her hair against the attitude of Simon who was embarrassed and offended by her presence. He breaks the Law and supports his disciples who broke the Law when that Law was oppressing ordinary people.
3. And when he himself is despised and marginalised because of his support for those on the margins, Jesus does not pull back or change his mind but continues, even to death, to stand up for and accompany those who were despised.

A truly liberating development

Taking our cue then from the dignity of all people, as a central defining theme of the Gospels, what are the principles of a development that is truly liberating.

- In the first place, development must not be **exclusive**, at least in the sense that the model of development that is being pursued must not *depend* on the exclusion of some. Some people cannot be discarded, written off or marginalised in order to achieve the development of the many. Still less can the many be discarded, written off or marginalised in order to achieve the development of the few.
- Secondly, the dignity of people demands that they **participate** in the decisions which are made about them and for them. The notion that some can make decisions for others is a denial of the right of people to make decisions about their own lives and development and to be in control of their lives. This of course is not to deny that some will have an expertise that is useful or even essential in reaching the best decision, but it does imply that decision-making must be made at as local a level as possible. Local knowledge, local commitment and local participation are key to authentic development. Ireland has, I think, the most centralised decision-making process in the Western world; the diminution of the powers of local government and the centralisation of all major decision-making in Dublin by a small number of elected representatives is something that must be fought. I believe that the most important contribution which the Church can make to political life in Ireland today, and to the pastoral needs of people, is to demand and fight for a political structure that decentralises decision making down to the local level. Such decentralisation will be fiercely resisted as it involves the transfer of power. Participation, then, at an appropriate level, in the decisions that shape and promote development are an essential ingredient if that development is to be authentic.
- The principle that no-one can be excluded for the sake of development of others has, as a consequence, that authentic development must be **sustainable**. Authentic development cannot poison the atmosphere, pollute the ground or exhaust non-renewable resources in a way that excludes future generations from an authentic development or perhaps even raises a question over their very survival.

• Authentic development must be **integral**. It cannot be solely understood in economic terms. We know that the mere accumulation of goods and services is not enough for the realisation of human development. But we often act as if it were. Today many in our society, though not all by any means, are caught up in a process of superdevelopment, which consists in the **excessive** availability of every kind of material goods. This superdevelopment has, as its goal, simply the multiplication or continual replacement of things already owned with others considered better. This civilisation of 'consumption' is characterised by so much waste.

• Finally, authentic development must be **self-reliant**. An inappropriate dependency on others, which is a consequence of a lack of participation in decision-making, makes any process of development insecure and fragile. It leaves people feeling like a pawn in the games of others, and as a cog in a machine that has been created to meet the needs of others. This is the very opposite of authentic development.

The role of culture
If authentic development is to take place, then the role of culture is very important. It is from culture that vision, energy and commitment come. Too often, culture is seen as irrelevant or even a hindrance to economic development – a backward influence which is to be overcome if true progress is to be achieved. However, culture is the bedrock on which solid development can take place. Authentic development has to respect the culture, build on the culture and certainly not destroy the culture.

Authentic development, then, must be inclusive, participative, sustainable, integral and self-reliant.

The question I am posing here is where do we, as Church, choose to put our energy?

Let us look then at models of development from the point of view of these criteria. Three models of development are dominant.

Models of development
The *economic model of development* is the one that Ireland is currently pursuing. It is based on attracting capital investment to

create jobs and increase output. The goal which it seeks to attain, its primary objective, is to increase the material standard of living of people and the measurement of success in achieving this goal is based on Gross National Product. The primary driving force for this model, the people who have to be cultivated, wooed, and licked up to, are business people.

Clearly, in recent years this model has been extraordinarily successful, within its own terms of reference and objectives. Success in achieving increasing material standards of living is also addictive so that any critique of this enterprise that we are pursuing is unwelcome. It is regarded as self-evident that this is the only way to proceed.

From the point of view of authentic development, there are several problems with this model of development. First, and most important, it is inherently based on the **exclusion** of many people; the products of those in Third World countries are subject to quotas, tariffs and other obstacles which make it very difficult for those who live there to achieve even a modest standard of living. It also excludes the many in our own country who are unable to get employment and who are condemned to poverty and to marginalisation. The last budget blatantly supported those who were in employment and gave the two fingers to those who were outside the workforce, including the old. The gap between those who are comfortable and those who are excluded grows bigger each year. It is simply not possible for this model of development to be inclusive. The standards of living of the select few (in world-wide terms) cannot be extended to everyone. We are beginning to face up to the impact on our present level of economic development of including Eastern European countries in the EU.

The second problem with this model of development is that it is **unsustainable**. If we were to try and extend this model to develop the standards of living of everyone, we would destroy the environment and our world.

This model of development is far from **integral**. There are more homeless on our streets than ever before, the gap between those who are comfortable and those on the margins continues to increase every year, and as crime, violence, drug misuse and insecurity become an increasing stress on all of our lives, the measurement of success in terms of material standard of living becomes ever more obviously inadequate.

This model of development is not **self-reliant**. Dependency on foreign multi-nationals whose core activities take place elsewhere in the world and without adequate linkages to the local economy is obviously not healthy from a long-term point of view. I think we recognise that today.

The current model of development is phenomenally successful in achieving its stated objective, but from a Christian point of view, the narrow focus on this objective is questionable.

If we, as Church, are to put our energy into pursuing and supporting this type of development, then we seek out entrepreneurs, mostly foreigners, cultivate them, and we give priority to forging relationships with them. We want their money to be invested in major projects which will create wealth and give employment. We are focused on the upper class who have the wealth. This is the primary path by which the development of the West will be achieved. Now, of course we need investment, of course we need entrepreneurs. But the question I am asking is, is this where we as Church are to put our energy?

The second model of development we might call *the social model of development*. It is based on a redistribution of resources. Its goal, its objective, is to create a more equal society, to ensure that all citizens participate more equally in the benefits which society produces. The primary driving force of this model are the politicians. Economic growth comes not just from capital investment, but also, and even more so from the harnessing of those human resources which on the economic model are effectively abandoned. By giving those outside the workforce an adequate, dignified standard of living, we can more easily release their energy, their initiative, their ingenuity and creativity.

The objective here is to ensure that the gap between the comfortable and those who are excluded is reduced by appropriate taxation and social welfare policies. Budget submissions, lobbying of Ministers for Finance and getting the support of local TDs and counsellors are the primary mechanisms for achieving this.

If we are to put our energy into this model of development, then the people we want to get at are politicians, local, national and European. Budget submissions and lobbying politicians are where we put our time and energy. In a sense, our focus in this strategy are the middle class, trying to secure agreement, or at least tolerance, for a redistribution of their income.

The third model of development we might call the *political model of development*. It focuses on the quality of growth, rather than the mere accumulation of material goods. It seeks to generate employment focused on meeting human needs rather than producing what advertising will encourage people to buy. It seeks to promote community participation. The key players in this model of development are grass-root social movements. If we put our energy into pursuing this model of development, then the people we work with are local communities. It is through the building up and empowering of local communities that development will come about. Local communities define the needs that are to be met and the response that must be made to achieve those needs. Local communities decide how to get the resources that are necessary and where they are to be sought. Local communities on their own, of course, are much less effective than if they are working together for a common end. Hence networking is a significant part of our work with communities. In the pursuit of this strategy, our focus is on ordinary people, and ordinary communities. This model essentially seeks a redistribution of power, rather than a redistribution of resources. It respects and builds on local culture. Local knowledge and local initiatives are the important ingredients in successful development.

The Church

If in bringing about change in society, we see it as necessary for that change to be participative, inclusive, integral, self-reliant, sustainable, then do we apply the same to the development of the Church?

Where do we put our energy in developing the Church? By analogy with the models of development of society, do we put our energy into wooing and influencing the Bishops, because they are the key people who wield power? Or do we put our energy into influencing and wooing the priests, the people on the ground whose decisions can affect whole communities? Or do we put our energy into forming and working with lay people as a strategy for bringing about change? If so, then we are essentially involved in a redistribution of power within the Church.

If we do not work for an inclusive, participative Church, then our work for an inclusive, participative development in society will be seriously compromised.

Ethics, Compassion and Self-Deceit

There is a homeless person sitting in the street, begging. Passing by, I wonder whether to give him money or not. On the one hand, I feel sorry for him, no place to go, hungry, cold, bored. On the other hand, maybe he isn't really homeless, or even if he is, maybe he wants money for drugs or alcohol and I may actually be making his situation worse by giving him money. It's all very confusing.

In the millennium, a sustained campaign was waged to abolish or reduce the debt owed by the poorest Third World countries, who were being crippled by the interest they had to pay on loans they had received from the economically developed world. The campaigners argued that this repayment was preventing health and education programmes from being funded and was therefore costing lives and preventing development. Others argued that corruption was so extensive in many of these countries and spending on arms and military so high that to simply cancel the debt would make their ruling elites even wealthier, their armies even better equipped and increase the oppression and suffering of the people, not reduce it. It's all very confusing.

Compassion
Unfortunately, ethical principles are not a quick-fix solution to our confusions. If they were, there would be no problems in the world. Ethical principles are grounded in the values of compassion and solidarity. What is absent in our world today is not a set of ethical guidelines but a deep sense of compassion and

solidarity. Unless a person is living those values, then ethical
principles become, not guidelines to just behaviour, but rules to be
manipulated, interpreted and twisted to one's own advantage.

Compassion is not a religious feeling. While it is central to
many religious faiths, including Christianity, compassion is a
human feeling that is innate in all of us. It is part of our humanity.
All of us, of whatever faith or none, are moved by the sight of
children starving, or being ill-treated. Cruelty and sadism shock us
all. We can, of course, become anaesthetised to suffering and
cruelty and there is a movement in that direction in our society.
Technology has enabled us to witness the suffering of so many
people in our world that we can sometimes close our eyes because
the pain becomes too much. We are also tempted to close our eyes
because we feel so powerless to do anything – there is nothing
worse than feeling pain at the suffering of another and knowing
that we can do nothing about it. Compassion involves a desire to
remove the pain from people's lives and give them a happier
future. But when the pain of observing the pain of others
becomes too much for us to bear, then we preserve our own sanity
by switching off. And so we have lost not so much our
compassion, but *our sense of outrage*. Homeless children on the
streets of Dublin in the year 2001, when our coffers were so full
that we could dream up National Stadiums on which to spend the
money, is an obscenity. We are all aware of children dying in our
world from hunger and preventable disease. But where is the
anger, where is the indignation, where is the sense of outrage?
Ethical principles are rooted in a deep sense of compassion. To act
ethically, we have to continually struggle against the tendency to
numb the pain of seeing others in pain.

Solidarity
Our sense of solidarity with others can help to prevent the
anaesthetic from dulling the pain. To empathise with another
person in their pain, to feel that pain as if it was our own, can help
to keep us alert to the suffering in the world. It is John and Mary
and Jane's pain, John, Mary and Jane being persons known to us,
which helps to minimise the tendency to treat the suffering of
others as merely a 'problem'. It helps to prevent the anonymity of

others, others being considered objectively as the 'clients' and the problem being 'an issue'. We need to get to know people who are poor, suffering and marginalised, to be able to see life through their eyes. People who are waiting years for an operation may see the budget in a very different way to those who are cushioned by their VHI payments. Preserving our sense of outrage through personal, direct contact with people who are poor, suffering or marginalised makes it more likely that we will act ethically towards the poor.

'Solidarity is not a feeling of vague compassion or shallow distress at the misfortunes of so many people, both near and far. On the contrary, it is a firm and persevering determination to commit oneself to the common good: that is to say, to the good of all and of each individual because we are all really responsible for all.' (Encyclical, *Social Concern*, par. 38).

Jesus did not pronounce ethical principles, he told stories about people.

> There was a rich man who used to dress in purple and fine linen and feast magnificently every day. And at his gate there lay a poor man called Lazarus, covered with sores, who longed to fill himself with the scraps that fell from the rich man's table. Dogs even came and licked his sores. Now the poor man died and was carried away by the angels to the bosom of Abraham. The rich man also died and was buried.
>
> In his torment in Hades, he looked up and saw Abraham a long way off with Lazarus in his bosom. So he cried out, 'Father Abraham, pity me and send Lazarus to dip the tip of his finger in water and cool my tongue, for I am in agony in these flames'. 'My son,' Abraham replied, 'remember that during your life good things came your way, just as bad things came the way of Lazarus. Now he is being comforted here while you are in agony. But that is not all: between us and you a great gulf has been fixed, to stop anyone, if he wanted to, crossing from our side to yours and to stop anyone crossing from your side to ours. (Luke 16:19-26)

The stories talked about situations in which people were treated badly, ignored or walked upon. The stories enabled people to empathise with others in the unjust situation in which they found themselves. The ethical thing to do was usually very clear, the ethical principles were deafeningly loud, but Jesus explained them in terms of concrete situations and real people. The discernment demanded by Jesus was based on compassion and solidarity.

'So always treat others as you would like them to treat you; that is the meaning of the Law and the Prophets' (Matthew 7:12)

Self-deception

Ethical principles also have to struggle against our almost infinite capacity for self-deception. Our ability to rationalise and make decisions, which are in our own interests, while preserving the belief that we are acting ethically, is usually very apparent in others! However, we can often delude ourselves that this very common phenomenon does not affect us. My desire for comfort or for security are two frequently occurring drives which affect my decisions. My attachment to my own way of doing things or my own attitudes and feelings about things may prevent me from being objective. This need for psychological security is particularly difficult to unmask as it may be rooted very deeply in my psyche and therefore very hidden even to myself.

Few of us are quite as transparent as President Bush, who is very clear that the national interests of the US should take precedence over everything else, including the environment, or Charlie McCreevy, Ireland's Minister of Finance during the Celtic Tiger years, whose understanding of social justice seems to be to support those who are doing very well. Most of us, however, are unwilling to admit that we are motivated by self-interest and believe that we are the essence of objectivity. The problem is not bad people making bad decisions, but good people making bad decisions having convinced themselves that they were good decisions. They are not acting out of malice – indeed it would be much easier to deal with if they were! – but out of ignorance, ignorance of the reality of life for poor people and of the effect of the decisions they make on their lives.

We see it in relations between different parts of the world, between different countries, different regions, different communities. Decisions that could make a vital, life-giving difference to some people are rejected, watered down or compromised because of the relatively minor effects or inconvenience which those decisions would have for those who make them.

A major part of the rationalisation which we all go on with is our unwillingness or inability to listen. We do not want our situation or our thinking to be disturbed by the contrary views of others. And so we set up mechanisms by which such challenges can be dismissed. We find all sorts of reasons which invalidate or rubbish such views. This is especially true of the views of the poor themselves, which of course challenge us the most.

In our society there are two (and indeed more than two) totally different views. There is the view of those who are in well-paid, secure, pensionable jobs, living in a nice house in a nice area and whose children are going to third-level education; and there is the view of those who are living on the fourteenth floor of a tower block in Ballymun where the lifts don't work, who have been unemployed for twelve years and whose children have dropped out of school and are hanging around with the wrong crowd. How they see the structures of Irish society and how they view the political, economic and social decisions that are made will probably be very different.

The perspective of the poor does not have any greater legitimacy than the perspective of any other group in our society or in our world. It is, like any other view, the view of a particular group who sees the world from their own unique situation. However, while it does not have greater legitimacy, it does have greater priority, simply because it is the view of those who are suffering or who have been excluded. This gives their viewpoint a uniqueness which demands particular attention. However, it often receives particular disdain – because they often lack education, and so they are written off as not having the knowledge to understand the 'complexity' of reality; or because they lack the literacy skills to present their views in a way that keeps decision makers happy; or because they are perceived to be biased because of their particular problems (as if the rest of us weren't!).

It is the difficult task of continually trying to listen to the views of those who are poor and excluded, of trying to see life through their eyes, which sustains our compassion and our solidarity. It is difficult because it challenges us, our viewpoint, our securities; sometimes it even accuses us. And we usually do not like to be challenged, still less accused.

Ethical principles have their place. But ethical principles tend to be enunciated by the rich and powerful. Unless they are enlivened and challenged by dialogue with the least powerful, and awareness of their problems, they become little more than maxims of self-interest. Acting justly does not depend on our understanding of ethical principles, helpful as that may be in some situations. It depends on the sort of person we are and are becoming.

Quality of Life

In 1999, the life of an Italian student, Mr Guido Nasi, who was visiting Ireland, was dramatically changed for the worse. His wallet had been stolen and he was wrestling with a young boy whom he suspected had taken his wallet. A passerby attacked him and struck him on the head with a half-full bottle of lager, which left him paralysed from the neck down. His assailant got eight-and-a-half years in prison. Now, his assailant certainly had no intention of causing such injuries to Mr Nasi. But to Mr Nasi, the intention of his assailant is irrelevant – the quality of his life has deteriorated dramatically as a result of his actions. Excuses do not undo the damage or make the pain go away. And the Court of Criminal Appeal had little sympathy for his assailant's excuses, as it confirmed the eight-and-a-half years sentence which he received because of his actions.

Every year, many victims of crime have their health and their security seriously damaged, and their fears increased, to such a point that they experience a significant deterioration in the quality of their lives. That those responsible for this deterioration did not intend to cause such a consequence is irrelevant to their victims.

Every year, many others, too, see the quality of their lives deteriorate, not as a result of criminal actions, but State inaction. The fact that the State did not intend to cause the quality of their lives to deteriorate is irrelevant to them. Like Mr Nasi, they have to suffer the consequences of the actions or inactions of others. Excuses do not make the pain any less.

- An endless succession of very damaged children have made their way to the High Court to plead for suitable accommodation, therapy, treatment and care. Some were suicidal, addicted, abused, trapped in prostitution. Their painful childhood experiences and memories were destroying their lives. They pleaded for help. Many were denied the help they needed. Some are now dead, some in prison, some destroyed by drugs.
- A fourteen year old with epilepsy, who had been raped, and had almost died from a drug overdose, failed to secure the appropriate therapy and treatment she needed. A fourteen year old, sexually abused by her father, and who had attempted suicide on Christmas day, was denied the help she needed.
- Judge Peter Kelly in another case before him, where the rights of the child had been breached for over three years, spelt out the consequences of failing to respond to their needs: 'The effect of the breach [of their rights] is one which, as a matter of high probability, will affect them into their future life and indeed may have fatal consequences for some of them.' So incensed was he by the excuses being given for their inaction, that he threatened to jail three Government Ministers for contempt of court.
- A young woman goes to casualty with severe abdominal pains. She is given an appointment for a scan in six weeks time.
- A four-year-old child who is going deaf because of an easily treatable condition has to wait a year for an appointment to see a specialist. Because he can't hear, his speech has not developed properly. He is on a long waiting list for speech therapy.
- A twelve-year-old boy, who had difficulty breathing, who woke up each night gasping because his mouth was so dry, waited five years to see a consultant to have his illness diagnosed and treated.
- A woman, suffering bouts of intense pain, suspected to be due to gall stones, waited eleven months to be examined by a consultant, waited a further six months to be seen by the surgeon and was *then* placed on a waiting list to be treated.
- While the Minister of Health rejects the word 'crisis' to describe what is happening to patients on waiting lists, a recent

statement from the Dublin Teaching Hospitals spelt out the consequences of delays in the treatment of the sick: 'consequent unnecessary morbidity because they cannot get into hospital – including disability, deformity and pain, with reduced quality of life.'

• Twenty-nine thousand people were on hospital waiting lists at the end of 2002, all suffering varying degrees of deterioration in the quality of their lives.

• Families with recently diagnosed children with disabilities have been placed on waiting lists for therapeutic or support services.

• Others, like Mrs Anne Lavelle, received letters earlier this year to say that there was no funding to provide services for their eighteen-year-old handicapped children once the school year ended.

• Mr Frank Conaty, Chairman of the Galway Alliance of Parents and Carers stated: 'Early childhood services are critical for people with disabilities as otherwise their conditions will just get worse ... I know of twelve families who have a newly-diagnosed child with an intellectual disability with absolutely nothing. As well as the effects on the child, I can't emphasise enough what that means for the parents. They are at the point where they are bankrupt emotionally and physically.'

• One parent of a young man with intellectual disability said in frustration: 'As parents we don't live in peace and, when we die, we don't die in peace, because there is no proper provision being made for our children.'

• Parents of almost 200 autistic children have had to go to the courts to get appropriate education for their children – they have often had to mortgage their homes, face lengthy delays, stressful litigation and the realisation that every day lost has implications for the long-term prospects of their children. They are often forced to give up employment to look after their children.

• More than 2,600 intellectually disabled persons have no services or have not received a diagnosis of their condition from health authorities.

• One young man with schizophrenia, who burns his arms with cigarettes, cuts himself with razors and hears voices, was discharged from a psychiatric hospital, to which he had been admitted two weeks earlier, with a note requesting the Homeless Persons Unit to try to find him emergency accommodation. This young man, incapable of looking after himself, was left to live on the streets. A recent Amnesty report stated that: '42 per cent (approximately 8,000) of homeless people are believed to have a history of mental health problems while a further 33 per cent are believed to suffer from severe mental and/or behavioural disorders which contribute significantly to their homeless state and are exacerbated by it.' As psychiatric patients in a service with very inadequate facilities, the quality of their lives is already very low. Add homelessness, and the quality of their lives drops to zero – or below.

Lives are being damaged, some destroyed, just as surely, and just as unnecessarily, as poor Guido Nasi's life. Excuses, political or economic, do not restore people's physical or mental health – or bring them back to life.

An Attempt at
Buddhist Meditation

During a two-month mini-sabbatical in South East Asia, I spent three weeks in a Buddhist monastery, attempting to meditate. I knew absolutely nothing about Buddhism (and still know very little), but what attracted me to try it was my vague understanding that their method of meditation was a very 'simple' form of meditation, – simple in the sense of 'uncomplicated' – that it sought to get beyond thoughts, concepts, ideas and mental images – more akin to silent contemplation than to meditation. So having decided that this would be the focus of my mini-sabbatical, then I had to decide where to go.

It was an Irish Jesuit colleague, working in Cambodia, who suggested that Thailand was my best bet – there are 32,000 Buddhist monasteries in Thailand! Surely one of them can provide me with what I want. I probably could have gone to the Buddhist community in Galway, but, with no disrespect to the people of Galway, Thailand seemed a little more attractive! So I turned to the Internet and found there (www.dharmanet.org/thai_94.html) a very detailed list and description of many of the monasteries in Thailand that provide meditation practice, including about a dozen who offer instruction in English. So I chose two, in the South of Thailand, which were close together (so if one was unavailable, I could try the other) and which did not require advance registration (allowing me maximum flexibility).

My first choice was a monastery on a small island twenty-five miles off the coast of Thailand. It was located on the top of a mountain so you had a magnificent view. The location determined my choice. It welcomed guests and offered meditation instruction in English. So off I went (slowly, of course, taking in a few beaches on the way) and eventually arrived to find that the English instructors were going off to Europe to teach meditation in two days time and the monastery was therefore unable to accept visitors! So my idyllic island monastery was not to be.

The second monastery was on the mainland, in the middle of a forest, so back on the boat I went to check it out. Sure enough, as I anticipated, it was offering a ten-day Buddhist retreat in English starting in a few days time. It was an international monastery in the sense that there was a monk from England, the US, Switzerland and Germany and one of their priority ministries was offering these ten-day Buddhist retreats each month in English to foreign tourists. It is a well-known monastery in Thailand, called Wat Suan Mokkh, founded by a very charismatic and highly revered monk who only died in 1993.

About ninety of us started the retreat – about sixty finished it. I was by far the eldest! Most of the group were young backpackers who were touring Asia for periods of between three months and ten years. They were almost all without any faith, but searching for something and hoping to find some direction in Buddhist meditation. Some were well qualified (a doctor, an architect, a diving instructor) and from time to time practised their skill to raise the money to travel. Others were students or early school-leavers who picked up odd jobs to raise the little income which they needed to live simply and travel.

The meditation technique
The meditation technique involved concentrating on the sensation of your breath as it passed in and out of your nostrils. This particular form of meditation (called *Anapanasati*) was considered by the monks there to be the purest form of Buddhist meditation and the technique taught by the Buddha 2,500 years ago.

The objective was to focus and concentrate the mind, getting rid of all thoughts, mental images, ideas and even feelings. As the mind becomes focused, it becomes calm. When your mind is sufficiently focused and calm, it can begin to understand how the mind works, which leads to wisdom, and wisdom, if lived out in daily life, leads to happiness.

Why do you focus on your breathing? Because I, breathing in and out, is the only thing that is real. Thoughts are about the past or the future – and the past is gone and the future is not yet. So thoughts cannot be the focus of our meditation. And feelings follow thoughts, so they too cannot be the focus of our meditation. So we attempt to get rid of thoughts and feelings to focus our mind on the here and now, the present reality, I, breathing.

We were expected to do about eight hours of meditation a day, for ten days (this was a relaxed monastery, many others expected up to twenty hours meditation a day). eight hours a day, for ten days, doing nothing but focusing on your breathing!

Does it work? The monks were the living proof that it does in fact work. They were extremely impressive men (and women, though Buddhist nuns are quite rare, but some lived in Wat Suan Mokkh), clearly people of great inner peace and calmness, full of kindness, patience and tolerance and living a life of extreme simplicity, even hardship.

Unfortunately, we shared the hardship! They – and we – slept on the stone floor, with only a straw mat to stop the cold coming up into our bones. Rise at 4am every morning (indeed it was hard to know which was worse, getting up at 4am or not getting up) and bed at 10pm. Breakfast at 8am, which consisted of rice and a banana, and lunch at 12.30, which consisted of rice, vegetables and a banana, and that was it. This was a rather relaxed monastery, as most monasteries only have one meal a day, which the monks have to beg for in the nearby villages or countryside. And the mosquitoes! I was eaten alive by mosquitoes. By the end of the third week, my wrists and ankles were swollen with so many bites. And Buddhism, some sections of which believe in reincarnation, has an absolute prohibition on consciously killing any living creature. I couldn't believe that this included mosquitoes, but it did.

The experience of meditation
What was the experience like? It was very difficult and even frustrating.

The *difficulty* was in getting rid of thoughts and feelings. Meditating on the air passing in and out of your nostrils is so incredibly boring that thoughts rush in to fill the vacuum. I just found it impossible to achieve. I was able to identify the moments when those thoughts flooded in – I could focus on my breathing in and I could focus on my breathing out, but the fraction of a second between the end of my in-breath and the beginning of my out-breath, and vice versa, were the moments when your concentration lapsed and allowed thoughts to enter. We were given instructions on how to get rid of thoughts: 'Gently put them away and return to your breathing. Do not force yourself' – I could hear my Jesuit Novice instructor of many years ago. But it was incredibly difficult to keep thoughts out for more than five minutes.

The *frustration* was in feeling that I was getting nowhere. Day after day, the thoughts and feelings came flooding in. Was I doing something wrong? Was I following the right technique? I was getting annoyed with myself. What advice was I given? 'Patient endurance'. That didn't seem very helpful. I was told to 'let go', to even let go of the desire to succeed, to let go of the frustration of getting nowhere. 'Just stay with it – patient endurance, and all will be well'. Had they no concrete advice to give? The answer was no. Learning to meditate was like learning to ride a bicycle, you have to learn by doing. You can listen to advice, you can watch demonstrations, but the only way to learn is to get up and do it for yourself. So it is in meditating that you learn how to meditate. I accepted it in blind faith. After day four, I certainly let go of the desire to succeed, because it was becoming painfully obvious to me that I wasn't going to succeed.

So what did it do for me? I became very aware, in an experiential rather than a cognitive way, of my human fragility. This particular, individual breath that I am inhaling is the difference between life and death. It may sound ludicrous, but I developed a relationship with each particular breath I took, I developed a respect and indeed, a reverence for, each breath, which held the power over me of life or death. I began to want not to lose the experience of a single breath, as each breath was such a vital part of me. The experience of my human fragility put everything into a different perspective. My plans, dreams, hopes – they were as fragile as myself. The future was very insecure – dependent on each single breath. This life-giving breath brought to mind some obvious biblical references – God breathing life into humanity at the beginning of creation, the Holy Spirit being given to the apostles.

What did I get out of it? I think the first thing that stayed with me was their emphasis on *living in the 'present'*. Concentrating on your breathing is not only a way of focusing the mind but is also intended to make you very aware of how you are in the present moment. It makes you very aware of the distinction between past, present and future and concentrates the mind, and feelings, on living in the present.

So when I feel frustrated, annoyed, angry, worried, upset – which might be me sitting in a traffic jam late for an appointment, or thinking about some future problem, or regretting something in the past – I try to focus on my breathing, remembering that the only reality is the present moment, and letting go of the frustration or worry about the past or future.

In Christian terminology, we might say 'the sacrament of living in the present moment'. I came to realise in a new way that so much of our unhappiness or dissatisfaction arises either from the past or from worry about the future and is so unnecessary. It became obvious to me that living in the present (which is not to say that we do not reflect on the past or plan for the future) is a necessary condition for attaining happiness. As the monks would say:

> If you worry, you die;
> If you don't worry, you die;
> So why worry?

The second thing that stayed with me was their emphasis on *'letting go'*. Buddhism seeks happiness, a happiness that nothing can disturb. True happiness, they believe, must be capable of being permanent or else it is not true happiness. Therefore it must be rooted in something permanent. Nothing which is transient can be the basis for such happiness precisely because it is transient. We so often seek happiness in having what we do not yet possess, (money, a bigger car, a foreign holiday, etc.) or in becoming what we are not yet (career advancement, more status in society, to be looked up to, etc.). But while such possessions or achievements might bring temporary satisfaction, we always move beyond them and search for something more or something new, precisely because they are 'impermanent'. From all the talks we had, perhaps the word 'impermanent' was the most frequently used and the word that stays with me. Nothing impermanent can give us the happiness we seek.

'The greatest obstacle to happiness is the search for happiness.' And so the path to happiness involves letting go of all that is 'impermanent'. This letting go is lived very radically by these Buddhist monks. Their lives are utterly simple. There was no physical comfort in the monastery (I often longed for a decent chair to flop into; the choice I had was a stone seat with no backrest or a sawn-off tree trunk). Letting go of thoughts, feelings, desires, emotions, goals, plans, projects and dreams was their objective. There was no ambition to be other than a simple monk, living in the present, meditating and studying the Buddhist scriptures. They were content with what they had and who they were. Looking at them from the viewpoint of my own Western culture and economic prosperity, it seemed they were so obviously on the right track. Reflecting on all the material possessions that I had, the opportunities I enjoyed, the prosperity that I took for granted, they all seemed, not just unimportant, but an actual obstacle to the attainment of a deeper inner peace. These monks in their simplicity and poverty radiated far more happiness and joy than I did. It just seems so obvious that a radical 'letting go' must be central to a spirituality for the Western world and yet we preach it so little and live it even less.

The third thing that stayed with me was their insistence that *the true source of happiness must be something permanent, unchangeable*. What is it, they asked, that is truly permanent and therefore can be the source of permanent happiness? For the Buddhist, it is 'The Law of Nature', understood as the 'way things, including the mind, work'. Happiness is going along with this law of nature, unhappiness is in opposing it, usually through ignorance. So understanding how the mind works, where our thoughts, feelings, desires, perceptions, emotions come from, and where they lead to, is the path to happiness. This understanding can only be attained by studying our own mind, through meditation. So the only unchangeable is the law of nature and happiness is achieved by knowing and flowing with this law.

For me, as a Christian, the unchangeable is 'the unconditional love of God.' This is the only unchanging reality in the universe and so it alone is capable of being the basis for a happiness that is permanent. Living in the knowledge of that love is the only true foundation for our joy. That love is permanent and unchanging and so our joy is secure. To try to base our happiness on anything other than the unconditional love of God is doomed to failure for everything else is changing or changeable, 'impermanent'. The more radical our letting go of all else, the firmer the foundation of our happiness becomes. If the foundation of our Christian joy is living in the knowledge that I, at this present moment, am loved unconditionally by God, then living in the present moment is the necessary pre-condition for experiencing this joy.

So, unfortunately, I didn't arrive at nirvana during my ten day retreat. In fact, I didn't arrive anywhere that was recognisable. So I stayed on for another ten days and did my own Jesuit retreat. Back to familiar territory, at last. The bed was still rock hard and the mosquitos still feasted on me but at least I knew what I was supposed to be doing.

And so I would describe myself as a failed Buddhist. But one of the benefits of being a failed Buddhist is that I may have to go back to South East Asia and try again!

Christmas Mass in Dóchas 2002

This piece was spoken at Midnight Mass in the Women's Prison

Think back to the first time you fell in love. Can you remember how you told the other person that you were madly in love with them? Of course you all said it in different ways, at different times and in different places. But one thing you all had in common – you told them *face to face*. You didn't send a mate to tell them – if you had sent a friend, they would rightly have wondered 'What's up, why couldn't they tell me themselves?' No, you went to them and told them yourself that you loved them. And then I'm sure you celebrated.

Tonight we celebrate God coming in person to tell us, face to face, how much God loves us. God didn't send messengers or angels to tell us, God came in person, to tell us.

This little child, his words, his life and his death, is God communicating to you how much you are loved.

> 'Can you not buy two sparrows for a penny? And yet not one falls to the ground without your Father knowing. Why, every hair on your head has been counted. So there is no need to be afraid; you are worth more than hundreds of sparrows.'
>
> 'As the Father has loved me, so I have loved you.'

This little child reveals a God whose love for you is so great that that neither your mind, nor even your unlimited imagination, can grasp how much you are loved. The love of God for you is infinite.

This little child reveals a love, which, from the moment you were created, is God's gift to you for life and for eternity. There is nothing and nobody who can take this gift away from you – not even yourself. Nothing can separate you from the love of God.

The love of God for you is unconditional.

But if tonight we rejoice and celebrate that night when God came to tell you and me that we are loved with an infinite and unconditional love, that's not the whole story. For in a few years time, this child will be executed. Why was Jesus put to death? You do not put to death someone who comes to tell you how much they love you!

No, Jesus had something else to tell us. He also told us, by his words and by his life and by his death, that God loves every other human being with the same infinite and unconditional love with which God loves me. And *that's* the problem.

The cranky neighbour whom I don't talk to, the person I can't stand, the person who has done me harm, those I don't want living beside me – this little child reveals that they too are loved by God as I am. And that has very radical consequences not only for my own behaviour towards others but also for the sort of society which we build. It is very appropriate that this celebration of God's love comes from this building, the women's prison. For you, along with others in our society, Travellers, homeless people, poor people, addicted people and others, are often stigmatised, unwanted, pushed aside, denied accommodation and treated like inferior human beings. Many want to hear about God's infinite love for *them*, but they don't want to hear about God's infinite love for *you*. Tonight we celebrate together that love during this hour in this Church; but we need also to leave here and to celebrate that love *every day in life*.

Some things have not changed since Jesus' day. Jesus got into a lot of trouble talking about God's love for other people – *some* other people. Two thousand years ago, he talked about, and revealed, God's love for prostitutes, tax-collectors and sinners. That upset some very important and respectable people. And some objected, they didn't want to hear *this*. So Jesus, God's revelation of love, was rejected and silenced. Today, Jesus is, again, rejected and silenced every time we exclude and marginalise groups or individuals in our society, no matter what excuse we use for doing so.

Tonight we celebrate God's extraordinary love for us. Our purpose in life is to grow into the likeness of God, the God who loves not only us but everybody else – without exception. Tonight's celebration is therefore also a challenge. Every time we welcome, reach out and accept those whom we would prefer to keep at a distance from ourselves, we grow more and more into the image and likeness of the God who loves all that God has created.

And so, tonight, rejoice, rejoice in the revelation of God's infinite and unconditional love for you, a bond of love that can never be broken, a gift of love, given to you to be shared with others – all others – without exception.

Homelessness and Exclusion

Those who say that people who are homeless are homeless by choice are quite correct – but it is a choice that someone else has made!

When the Minister for Finance during the Celtic Tiger years was receiving a lot of criticism over the cost of accommodating the rapidly growing number of asylum seekers, he replied, without apparently realising the irony of his remark: 'Well, what do you want us to do? Let them live on the streets?' When available accommodation seemed to be inadequate to house the growing number of asylum seekers, advertisements appeared in all the papers seeking suitable privately-owned accommodation. Some hotels and other accommodation centres were purchased, others were rented. When this proved insufficient, the Government bought mobile homes and placed them on Government-owned sites, with electricity and sewage provided, which accommodated 1,000 asylum seekers. Pre-fabricated system-built homes were provided to accommodate a further 4,000. Sites of 1.5 acres or more were sought which could provide further accommodation. Accommodation was required for some 8,000 asylum seekers in 2001 alone, and accommodation was found for every single one of them.

This is not to suggest that asylum seekers are being pampered by our Government while homeless people are being ignored. Indeed, in many respects, asylum seekers and refugees have a lower quality of life and less legal protection even than our own homeless people. It is simply to suggest that the plight of homeless people is not due to circumstances over which we have no control. The difference between asylum seekers who require accommodation and homeless Irish people who require accommodation was that the political will exists to solve one problem but not the other. The Minister for Justice made a decision and asylum seekers were accommodated. Homeless people still await a similar decision from the Minister for the Environment.

Some say that 'a rising tide lifts all boats'. But those who are homeless don't even have a boat. Their plight is not automatically changed with changing economic circumstances. For over a decade, Ireland experienced very difficult economic times, with very high long-term unemployment and poverty. During this period, the number of homeless, not surprisingly, increased significantly. In more recent times, with the Irish economy growing at an unprecedented pace, the rise in property values, and consequently the increase in demand for rented accommodation with a disproportionate increase in the rentals being demanded, the numbers of homeless have increased even further. In good times and in bad, those who are homeless continue to be homeless and their numbers continue to increase, unless decisions to remedy their plight are made by others, to whom they have no access.

Homeless people, then, are people who have been *excluded*. And so the hardest part of being homeless is not the physical discomfort, or the boredom, but living, every moment of every day, with the knowledge that you are not considered valuable, worthwhile or important enough for someone to make a decision that you should have what the rest of us take for granted, a place of your own. To be considered of so little value is to have your dignity undermined or taken away. Homeless people have to struggle to maintain their sense of their own dignity, in the face of the contrary message which their status proclaims and communicates to them on a daily, even hourly, basis. Homeless children are particularly damaged by their homelessness. Their sense of their own identity is still being formed, their perception of themselves and of the society around them is still being moulded. To live in the knowledge that that society considers them to be nobody and does not appear to care about their homelessness is to create an adult with little or no self-respect and a lot of anger. That combination of emotions is dangerous. Is it surprising that some homeless people turn to drink or drugs to suppress their negative feelings? And that the final outcome may well be a sudden death from drugs or suicide or at best an early death from ill-health and premature old age.

Homelessness in Ireland has changed in nature over the last few years. In the first place it has increased rapidly in very recent years. The Simon Community estimates that 10,000 adults are now homeless in Ireland, compared to 5,000 in 1993. There are two broad categories of homeless people:

- Those for whom poverty, combined with a crisis such as eviction or breakdown in relationship, has created a situation where the person cannot afford private housing and is not eligible, at least for a long time, for public housing.
- Those who have chronic personal problems.

In this second group, there are a large number of young homeless, who are drug using, and who are intimidating to the traditional, older homeless men and women for whom hostels had become their home. These older men and women move out to sleep on the streets and the hostels can no longer depend on the goodwill of volunteers to staff them. They now require experienced, trained and well-paid staff to cope with the difficult, disruptive behaviour of many of those who now use them. These younger, difficult homeless people have often suffered appalling traumas in their childhood, such as violence, sexual abuse, lack of love or care; some of them were introduced to drugs or alcohol by their parents at a very early age; some tried to 'parent' their parents who were often too drunk or stoned to look after themselves. This illustrates the fact that homelessness is often not just about having nowhere to live, but also involves a multiplicity of other problems – medical, psychological, psychiatric, addiction, low self-esteem, poor relationship skills – which, if not adequately dealt with, make it impossible to maintain accommodation, even if it is made available.

Many of those in the first category above are unwilling or afraid to accept the offer of accommodation in hostels. They may find themselves sleeping next to a drug user, or they may be robbed of what little they have, or be offered drugs, or sexually molested. Homeless people who are not streetwise do not usually have suitable accommodation available to them, as the shortage of accommodation makes assessment of needs a pointless exercise.

In the past few years, the newly-formed Homeless Agency has tried to ensure a more co-ordinated and therefore more effective response to the plight of homeless adults. Their vision is to eliminate homelessness by the year 2010 and to minimise the risk of people becoming homeless by the provision of effective preventative policies and services. The values that have informed their plan are worth mentioning, because they are values that are often not applied by policy-makers, or even by the public, to homeless people:

- Homelessness is solvable and preventable.
- Homelessness has as much to do with social exclusion as with bricks and mortars.
- Every household is entitled to a place they can call home which is secure and appropriate to their needs and potential.
- People who become homeless are entitled to services of the highest quality.
- Each person is unique and must be valued as such.
- People who become homeless have the right to be treated with dignity and respect and to have their beliefs and choices respected.
- People who are homeless should be involved in decisions that affect them.

Their plan, covering 2001 to 2003, is specific, detailed, comprehensive and multi-faceted. It has a total of 113 objectives covering all aspects of a homeless person's life, and includes:

- The provision of a twenty-four-hour free phone service, providing advice, information and referral, targeted at people who are homeless or at risk of homelessness.

- The provision of at least one hundred additional places in emergency and other hostel accommodation for street homeless people
- The provision of an additional 240 hostel places for emergency accommodation.
- The provision of 200 units of transitional housing targeting a mix of families and single people in the Dublin area.
- The provision of 300 additional units of long-term supported/sheltered housing for single homeless people and a further 1200 additional units of long-term housing.

For decades the problem of homelessness has been ignored. Now, under the inspired and inspiring leadership of Mary Higgins, its director, the Homeless Agency has been established and after much time, effort and consultation has produced a detailed, targeted plan which is capable of effectively solving the problem of homelessness. The test, of course, is ultimately whether its targets are met. This depends on the decisions that people make. Homeless people will have to wait and see. Unfortunately, it appears that the targets for the provision of accommodation sought in the three-year plan are, despite the best efforts of the Homeless Agency, hopelessly behind schedule. While this is depressing, it is hardly surprising. Homeless people have learnt from experience not to expect much.

In the past, there were two major exits out of homelessness for those who found themselves in that situation: the first was through the private, rented sector. Homeless people, with financial support from the Health Board or the voluntary sector, paid a deposit on a flat and a weekly rent. This exit is now virtually blocked off. Due to the Celtic Tiger, many people have returned to this country and others have arrived here to seek employment and most of them seek accommodation in the private rented sector. The queues for every vacant flat are three times longer than normal and landlords will rarely pass over a person who is working and has the money in their hand in order to accept a homeless person who is unemployed and pays with a welfare cheque. The second exit was through the Local Authority. But again, this exit has almost entirely been blocked off. Due to the

Celtic Tiger, the price of property has made it impossible for many middle-income families to afford a mortgage and so the waiting lists for Local Authority accommodation have increased dramatically. Homeless people, particularly single homeless people, are pushed to the back of the queue with no chance of ever seeing the key to their own front door. Thus homeless people depend on decisions that private landlords, or managers in City Councils, or Government Ministers make, if they are to succeed in exiting from homelessness.

However, as always in the past, there is more than a strong possibility that homeless people will, once again, be left at the bottom of the pile.

When we look at the problem of homeless children, we have a very different situation. Unfortunately, the only similarity with homeless adults is that the problem of homeless children has also been ignored by the political and social services for decades. It was not just the failure to provide the finances to support the services needed; there were, and continue to be, major structural problems in the current provision of services.

How does the system work? On the ground, homeless children access services through their local social worker. The social services are understaffed and social workers are therefore overworked. They have to prioritise. Their priorities are, rightly, very young children and children who have been, or who are alleged to have been, sexually abused. The mindset of social workers is, rightly, child protection. Hence, when a sixteen year old, with a cigarette hanging out of his/her mouth, comes into the office to say that their mother has thrown them out of the house, it hardly ranks as a priority. The duty social worker will listen, take the details, and ask the young person to seek accommodation from the emergency, overnight, service. When the young person returns to see the duty social worker some days later, they will almost certainly meet a different social worker and have to tell their story all over again. Week after week, they return to see the social worker and may meet different social workers on each visit. Social workers are so overworked that no-one is available to be allocated to them as their own. They often feel like a number, not a person with a problem that someone is interested in. Many express very negative feelings about social workers. This is not the social workers fault; they are overworked and over-stressed. Many of them do more than their best for young homeless people. But the young person needs someone to give them time, to listen, to support them, to help them to deal with the crises they have been through. And time is often the one thing that social workers cannot give.

At a higher level, there are too many middle managers within the social services and abundant anecdotal evidence that often they do not listen to their social workers on the ground. There is a high level of frustration amongst social workers who work regularly with homeless young people. They often feel that their concerns are not being heard or adequately addressed.

At the top, there are three Ministers who all may have some responsibility for homeless children. If at 9.00am, a homeless child is arrested for shoplifting and brought to the Children's Court, that child is then the responsibility of the Minister for Justice. If they are remanded in custody at 11.00am, they become the responsibility of the Minister for Education. If the Juvenile Detention Centre is full and they cannot be accepted, at 12.00 midday they become the responsibility of the Minister for Health – all in the one morning! This division of responsibility leads to 'passing the buck' and young homeless people get caught in the middle with a less than adequate service.

The establishment of the Forum on Youth Homelessness in 1999, under the chairmanship of Dr Miriam Hederman O'Brien, by the former Eastern Health Board was a serious attempt to improve the structure within which services to homeless children were delivered. The Forum produced its Report in March 2000 and presented it to the Eastern Regional Health Authority, the successor to the Eastern Health Board.

The Forum was very critical of the current structures which existed to serve the needs of homeless young people. In particular, it criticised the absence of any plan to deal with the problem and the ad-hoc response to crises which characterised management's approach. It recommended a radically new approach – creating an Independent Board, a Director with responsibility for the issue of homeless children, increasing the age of young homeless people whose needs are being met by these new structures from eighteen to twenty, the creation of locally-based multidisciplinary teams to work with homeless young people and the establishment of inter-linked residential placements which would provide much greater flexibility in meeting the needs of homeless young people.

In summary, the Forum recommended:

- *The designation of* **one authority** *to have statutory responsibility for the delivery of services to young people, aged twelve to twenty, who are out of home – this may involve the establishment of a new executive authority.*
- *A* **Board** *with responsibility for the effective planning, delivery and monitoring of services for young people aged between twelve and twenty out of home, should be established. It should be chaired by an independent person and have a maximum of twelve members. It should include people with relevant experience of the funding, delivery and co-ordination of services for young homeless people. It should also include members of statutory and voluntary services, and service users. It should be the conduit for all statutory funds to the various agencies. It should have its own budget and be responsible for the discharge of its obligations*
- *A* **Director** *responsible to the Board for a range of duties, including the preparation of short-term and longer-term plans, research and the co-ordination and delivery of appropriate, integrated services should be appointed.*
- **Interlinked groups of residential units**, *family placement and ancillary services should be established. They should be flexible, localised and co-ordinated.*
- *The designation of* **(multi-disciplinary) teams**, *which would include professionals from a range of different disciplines, to work with young people out of home or at risk of homelessness in the community.*

Despite public assurances that all the recommendations of the Forum Report were being accepted by the Eastern Regional Health Authority, the reality is that the new structures envisaged by the Forum have, in fact, been almost completely rejected. A Director of Homelessness has been appointed, but her brief is homeless adults as well as homeless children and she does not have the role or responsibilities or authority envisaged by the Forum. Multi-disciplinary teams are being created but they are not the locally-based response which the Forum considered necessary. No change in the structure of single, 'stand-alone' residential units has been proposed. The upper age remains eighteen years of age. The Independent Board has been flatly rejected. The same system, which has not only failed to eliminate youth homelessness over the past twenty years but has seen the problem relentlessly increase, continues to be given responsibility for dealing with the problem.

In October 2001, a Youth Homeless Strategy was published by the Department of Health and Children. It required the Health Boards to develop, within three months, a two-year strategic plan to eliminate youth homelessness in their areas. The Strategy was excellent. However, the data on which a comprehensive plan would be based exists only in a very inadequate, and sometimes inaccurate, form. Data in relation to the numbers of homeless children, the areas they come from and their needs is in short supply. It was difficult to see how a comprehensive and detailed plan could have been produced.

However, the Youth Homeless Strategy was the first attempt to seriously deal with the problem. It sought to eliminate youth homelessness within two years. It demanded that the Health Boards produce their plans to do so. Homeless children, like homeless adults, must wait and see.

The 'common good' takes precedence over private, vested interests. It is the role of Government to promote the 'common good' and to ensure its priority over private interests. That each person should have a place that we can call home is a right that most of us take for granted. We would find it intolerable that we should be left to sleep on the street. But when those who are appointed or elected to promote the 'common good' find that their own private interests are in conflict with the decisions which the 'common good' require, then people will be left excluded. In 1967, the Kenny report on land in urban areas recommended that all land in the vicinity of urban areas should be purchased by the Local Authority at its current value plus twenty-five percent. The

Local Authority could then utilise the land in the interests of the 'common good'. Although the report was chaired by a High Court Judge, the Government of the day decided that such a recommendation would be unconstitutional. In hindsight, it is clear that such a recommendation conflicted with the private interests of those in Government and their friends in the construction industry. The result is that today accommodation for those on low incomes is very scarce and people remain homeless.

Apart from the right to life, which is in a category all of its own, the fundamental human rights are: the right to adequate food, the right to a basic education, the right to a place called home, the right to basic health care and the right to work. Each of these rights are denied to some people in Irish society. They are excluded from the very fabric of society. A just society is one which ensures that each citizen has their fundamental rights guaranteed by law and provided through the structures of the state, and which seeks to ensure that the private, vested interests of individuals cannot obstruct the fundamental rights of others. In the Ireland of the Celtic Tiger and after, some are unfortunately going in the opposite direction.

The Giver of Gifts

'Give us a sign'

Sometimes my faith grows dim. Sometimes I wonder is there a God at all or are we all just fooling ourselves. When I get up there, I will have a question for God: 'If it is so important that we believe in you, why did you make it so difficult for us? Could you not have done a little parting of the Liffey waters from time to time, just to prove that you existed? Then people could have said: "I know God exists, I have seen the sign"' I sympathise with the authorities in Israel who, when Jesus came and said that he was from God and had a revelation from God, asked him to give them a sign that he was who he said he was. 'If you are the Son of God turn these stones into bread and we will believe you'. And again, 'If you are the Son of God, throw yourself down from this tower and the angels will bear you up and you will not be harmed – and then we will believe you.' And what does Jesus say? 'No sign shall be given to this generation'. I always thought that that was most unreasonable of him – why did he have to make it so difficult for them? The least he could do was to give them a little sign.

In fact, the signs are all around us, but we cannot see them. Jesus too was giving signs all the time, but they couldn't read them. But that is for later.

The Giver of the Gifts

There are times when I need to be alone, to be away from all this hectic activity, surrounded by people, demands and noise. I imagine myself to be swimming on a lake, a crowded lake, adults and children all competing for a little share of the water. Where can I just be alone for a moment? I have to dive beneath the surface, deep down into the lake, as far as I can go, until I stand on the rock, unable to go any further. In those depths of the heart, where nothing disturbs the silence and no light or movement to distract you, I am all alone with myself – and my memories. My memories of childhood, family life, adolescence, happy times, even sad times, from which you emerge stronger, wiser, more cautious – memories of gifts received and opportunities given – these are my companions in the deep. At these depths, all is experienced as gift. I feel a great sense of gratitude, gratitude for everything that I have received. I have nothing, I am nothing that was not gift. My very being, my family, my health, my intelligence, everything is gift. My gratitude reaches out to the Giver of the Gifts.

The gifts I recognise as gifts given only on loan. Over time, all these gifts will be taken back. My life is one long letting-go. At birth, I let go of the security of my mother's womb; through childhood and adolescence I let go of my dependency on my parents; in time, I let go of my parents, as they let go of life; in old age, or earlier, I let go of health, perhaps of mind; and eventually I let go of life itself. What right have I to complain? These gifts were given freely and now they are asked for back. They belong to the Giver of the Gifts, they were only given on loan.

But at these depths, I am conscious of one other gift, a gift that comes with each of the gifts I have received, but yet is independent of them, a gift that is given, not on loan, but for ever. It is the gift of being loved, of being loved by the Giver of the Gifts. When all the gifts have been given back, the gift of being loved remains.

At these depths, I experience the joy of being loved, loved infinitely and unconditionally, by the Giver of the Gifts.

I am loved *infinitely*. The Giver of the Gifts wishes me to be happy. Every parent wants to give their child all the happiness which they are capable of giving to them. The Giver of the Gifts will not withhold any happiness from me. Infinite happiness is my destiny. And so I am loved infinitely.

It is this love that gives me my value. I am like a Picasso painting: a Picasso painting, valued at fifty million euro, where does its value come from? It comes from *outside* itself. Its value is *given* to it. It is valued at fifty million because others give it that value, others love it to that extent. But although its value comes from *outside* itself, its value resides *in* the painting itself. If I put an exact, identical copy of the painting beside it, the copy has little or no value. The value is *in* the Picasso painting, but the value is given to it from *outside* itself.

And so my value comes from outside myself, from the infinite love which the Giver of the Gifts has for me. But although the value comes from outside myself, the value belongs to *me* – I am of infinite value. I have this unsurpassable dignity, which has been given to me.

And I am loved *unconditionally*. Nothing can separate me from the love of God, The one thing in this world that never changes is God's love. And so no-one, nothing, not even my own sinfulness, can take away, or reduce, the value and dignity that God's love bestows on me.

This conviction, that I am loved infinitely and unconditionally, is the foundation stone of our commitment to justice. Because if I am loved infinitely and unconditionally, then *so is everyone else*. If I have this infinite dignity, then *so has everyone else*.

This conviction is a challenge to our culture, which seeks to give value to people by what they do, what they achieve, how they succeed. Our culture seeks to value people by what comes *out* of them; our faith seeks to value people by the love of God, which has been put *into* them.

The signs

And so when I go before my God and ask my question: 'Why did you not give us a sign?' I imagine God will answer: 'You foolish human being. Do you not know who I am? I am not a magician. I am your Father and your Mother. Do not stand looking up into the sky to find me. Look to your right and look to your left. There you will see my children, many of them suffering, many lonely, many unwanted, many rejected – their dignity as children of mine has been taken away from them. My concern, as you should have realised, because many of you too are parents, my concern is my children. Reach out to them, and they will lead you to me.'

When Jesus, in his time, was asked for a sign, he too refused to become a magician. But one person asked for a sign and got it. That was John the Baptist. John, from his prison cell, sent his messengers to Jesus with the question: 'Are you the one who is to come or have we got to wait for someone else?' (Matthew 11:3) In other words, give us a sign. And what does Jesus say? 'Go back and tell John what you hear and see: the blind see again, and the lame walk, lepers are cleansed and the deaf hear and the dead are raised to life and the Good News is proclaimed to the poor; and happy the man who does not lose faith in me'. (Matthew 11:4-6) In other words, the signs that Jesus was from God were the *signs of compassion*. Jesus was trying to say: 'Miracles prove nothing – every generation has its magicians! But if you knew who God was, if you knew that our God is a God of compassion, then you would recognise that I am from God by the signs of compassion that I do. If you do not recognise that I am from God, then you do not know God.'

We look at a child in the pram and we say: 'Oh, he's lovely, he's the image of his father/mother.' We recognise that the child is the child of their parents because we see in the child's features the same features that we recognise in the parent. So Jesus was trying to say: 'The only way to know whether I have come from God is if you see in me the same likeness that you find in the Father'. If our God is a God of compassion, the only way we can recognise the Son of God is by the Son's compassion. And if our God is a God of compassion, the only way we can recognise the disciple of God is by the disciple's compassion.

So when my faith grows dim, where do I go to have my faith restored? Moving statues? Forget it. What sort of God would have even the remotest interest in playing games with statues? When my faith grows dim, my faith is restored by the countless acts of compassion of innumerable people who are reaching out to the sick, to the lonely, to the poor, the depressed and the marginalised, to the dying and the unwanted. There I find the evidence that God exists in our world.

And when the faith of others grows dim, I hope that they can find, in our compassion to others, the signs that God still works in our world. If we do not reveal the face of God to others, then God remains hidden from their sight.

Link between faith and justice

The link, then, between faith and justice is the *dignity* of people. We could sum up the whole Gospel by saying that Jesus came to proclaim that God is the Parent of every human being; and conversely that every human being is a child of God and has the dignity of being a child of God.

But if our faith proclaims in *words* the dignity of every human being, then our commitment to justice seeks to make that dignity a *reality* for every human being. Faith without justice is hypocrisy – it is empty words that mean nothing because we have taken the meaning out of them. Justice seeks to put that meaning back into the words, to make reality reflect what we say, and what we say to reflect reality.

And so compassion is the heart and soul of justice; it is the beginning, the middle and the end of our commitment to justice. Our reaching out to those whose dignity is being denied or threatened by the way in which they are treated by society, is the meaning and the content of our struggle for justice.

Motivation for our commitment to justice

Why do I commit myself to this reaching out, which can be difficult, self-sacrificing and problematic?

Is it for the sake of the reward, the Kingdom of God? No. Because there is no reward. We have already been given the Gift of the infinite love of God, and that Gift is ours to keep for ever. God has nothing else to give us; there is nothing more that we can receive. There is no other reward, beyond what we already possess. The Kingdom of God is already ours.

Is it for fear of punishment, if I fail to show love? No. The justice of God is fulfilled in forgiveness. God sets right the relationships, which our sinfulness has distorted, not by seeking vengeance but by forgiveness. The unconditional love of God always forgives us our failings.

So why do I seek to do the will of God, which can be difficult and problematic if it is not to gain some reward or avoid some punishment?

The only motivation is *gratitude*, gratitude for the gifts which I have received, and for the Gift which comes with the gifts, the infinite and unconditional love given by the Giver of the Gifts. The deeper my appreciation of that love, the deeper my gratitude and the more I am committed to reaching out to God's children on the margins. And the more I reach out to God's children on the margins, the closer they lead me to the Giver of the Gifts. So the foundation stone for justice is my appreciation of, and gratitude for, that love of God.

Union with God through compassion

'Jesus took with him Peter and James and his brother John and led them up a high mountain by themselves. There in their presence he was transfigured: his face shone like the sun and his clothes became as dazzling as light. And suddenly Moses and Elijah appeared to them; they were talking with him. Then Peter spoke to Jesus. 'Lord,' he said, 'it is wonderful for us to be here; if you want me to, I will make three shelters here, one for you, one for Moses and one for Elijah.' He was still speaking when suddenly a bright cloud covered them with shadow, and suddenly from the cloud there came a voice which said, 'This is my Son, the Beloved; he enjoys my favour. Listen to him.' When they heard this, the disciples fell on their faces, overcome with fear. But Jesus came up and touched them, saying, 'Stand up, do not be afraid.' And when they raised their eyes they saw no one but Jesus.'

A long tradition in spirituality identified the search for union with God as being found in contemplative prayer. In that tradition, it was understood that we can only unite ourselves with God through uniting our *spirit* with God, who is Spirit. This means leaving behind this material, messy, chaotic world and climbing the mountain, with Peter, James and John, in search of God. There, at the top of the mountain, far distant from the cares of this world, in those highest forms of contemplative prayer, we enter into an intimate relationship with God. Like Peter, James and John, we wish to remain there and enjoy the intimacy. In that intimacy, traditional spirituality understood, we find union with God.

However, St Ignatius, the founder of the Jesuits, had a different understanding of how we find union with God. Yes, he would say, climb the mountain; yes, enter into that intimate relationship with God at the highest levels of contemplative prayer; yes, experience the joy of that intimacy. But no, you may not remain there. You have not yet found union with God. To find union with God, you must go back down the mountain, return to this material, messy, violent world, and there you will find union with God, through *union of your will with God's will*. And the will of God, who is compassion, is that we, too, be compassion. In our compassion, we become like God; in our compassion, we become one with God; in our compassion, we find union with God.

So as I leave, for a time, the children of God on the surface of the lake, to be alone at the bottom of the lake with myself, my memories and my God, I feel the desire to return to the surface, and there, in gratitude, return a gift to God. The gift that God, our Parent, most desires is that we reach out to God's children, remove their pain and bring them joy. In our solidarity with God's children, we discover who God is, and in finding God, we find ourselves.